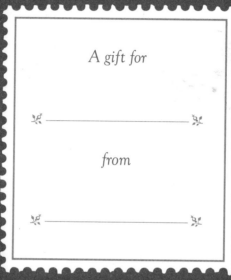

A gift for

⚹ ─────────────── ⚹

from

⚹ ─────────────── ⚹

Green *and* Pleasant Land

―ᴡᴡ―

Best-Loved Poems of the
British Countryside

By the same author:

The Book-Lovers' Companion: What to Read Next (Ed.)

I Wandered Lonely as a Cloud… : and other poems you half-remember from school (Ed.)

Tyger Tyger Burning Bright: Much-Loved Poems You Half-Remember (Ed.)

Poems to Learn by Heart (Ed.)

ANA SAMPSON

Green *and* Pleasant Land

Best-Loved Poems of the
British Countryside

MICHAEL O'MARA BOOKS LIMITED

For Isabelle and Poppy, the youngest poetry lovers I know.

First published in Great Britain in 2014 by
Michael O'Mara Books Limited
9 Lion Yard
Tremadoc Road
London SW4 7NQ

A CIP catalogue record for this book is available from the British Library.

Papers used by Michael O'Mara Books Limited are natural, recyclable products
made from wood grown in sustainable forests. The manufacturing processes
conform to the environmental regulations of the country of origin.

ISBN: 978-1-78243-301-9 in hardback print format

1 3 5 7 9 10 8 6 4 2

Designed and typeset by www.glensaville.com
Cover design by Claire Cater

Cover illustration: 'The South Downs' S.R. Poster, 1946
© NRM/Pictorial Collection/Science & Society Picture Library

Printed and bound by CPI Group (UK) Ltd, Croydon, CR0 4YY

www.mombooks.com

Contents

Introduction

The British are not the only nation who eulogize the beauties of their landscape, nor were we even the first. The Ancient Greeks praised the shepherd's life – Arcadia was simply a rural region of Greece before it came to symbolize a mythic idyll where Pan cavorted with herdsmen. However, it is fair to say that the British pastoral tradition has proved particularly fertile and enduring. We are an island at the mercy of unpredictable weather, as anyone who has attended a garden barbecue or music festival in Britain will confirm. Yet the British have long believed in the spiritual dividends to be derived from nature. We treasure our magnificent views. We ramble. We flock in our thousands to our country's cherished wildernesses, from the Lake District to the Dales and from the Highlands to Snowdonia.

Sixteenth-century poets celebrated the verdant countryside. *The Faerie Queen's* allegorical quest wends its way through a recognizably English fairyland. Shakespeare, darling of the London stage, betrays his Warwickshire roots with the gorgeous accuracy of his lines on wild thyme and autumn leaves. In the seventeenth century, poets rhapsodized about a rustic life away from cut-throat court politics and Civil War, albeit one also far removed from the reality of backbreaking toil, knee-deep in manure. Eden appears frequently as a very British garden, as poets fail to imagine a land more beautiful than their own.

By the second half of the eighteenth century, in the wake of the urban Enlightenment, the Romantics were turning back to nature. The countryside was a powerful inspiration as the Lake Poets and those that followed were moved to giddiness by sublime vistas. There emerged a tendency to idealize the peasant life – actually one of grinding poverty – which strikes an odd note now, but the rhapsodies of Wordsworth and his contemporaries have undoubtedly been absorbed into the British cultural identity.

At times of crisis, and during increasingly secular eras, nature is a talisman. Wistful poems celebrating the countryside flooded out of the First World War trenches, as soldiers mired in mud dreamed of Blighty and remembered their childhoods among her meadows and rivers. Rupert Brooke and Edward Thomas – both lost in the slaughter – represent this nostalgic strand of writing here. Later, poets lamented the threat posed to rural Britain by the march of modernization, though this was far from a new theme. Wordsworth and Manley Hopkins, among others, had mourned the city's sprawl into the countryside long before Betjeman, the twentieth century's great champion of provincial England, wrote in this vein.

The British notion of childhood is inextricably linked with the idea of the countryside. Our children's literature boasts only a handful of urbanites and a disproportionate amount of messing about on boats. Few British schoolchildren escape muddy walks, and an unshakeable belief in the benefits of healthy fresh air is built into the national psyche. Poetry is an escape hatch, parachuting us into pleasure from our hectic lives, so it is little surprise that poets frequently whisk us off to an often apocryphal carefree country childhood.

I was surprised, while researching this anthology, how many of the poets featured were city dwellers and, specifically, Londoners. Chaucer, Marlowe, Pope and Keats are among the dozens gathered here. Literary life has been centred on the capital for much of the nation's history, but perhaps the town dweller's thirst for natural beauty is more powerful for being unquenched. The pastoral was always a genre that romanticized its subject: by townies, for townies, it was aimed at a literate urban audience rather than the swains and milkmaids it portrayed. Many of the poems gathered in these pages were written abroad, too: Shelley, Keats and the Brownings were all in Italy when they wrote verses that still encapsulate the British landscape to readers today. Home-thoughts from abroad are, perhaps, all the sweeter.

I apologize as always for omissions and for the fact that some poems cannot be reproduced in their entirety for reasons of space. I do hope that wherever you are when you dip into this book, you will benefit from a quick blast of healthy fresh air and a dose of the beauty that has soothed, inspired and nourished so many of our greatest writers throughout the centuries. I offer you my guarantee that within these pages you will find the quickest route into the British countryside that exists. Happy rambling!

Ana Sampson
London, 2014

GREEN AND PLEASANT LAND

The myriad beauties of our nation's landscapes have awed and inspired our greatest poets for centuries, moving them to put pen to paper and pay tribute to the land they love. This section sees some of our best-known wordsmiths celebrate the country's natural splendours.

William Blake (1757–1827)

Extract from Milton – Jerusalem

Blake was born and bred a Londoner, but this iconic verse – now the nation's best-loved hymn – was composed in Felpham, Sussex, where he lived for a time with his wife. They are known to have scandalized neighbours by conducting naked reading sessions in the garden.

And did those feet in ancient time
Walk upon England's mountains green?
And was the holy Lamb of God
On England's pleasant pastures seen?

And did the Countenance Divine
Shine forth upon our clouded hills?
And was Jerusalem builded here
Among these dark Satanic Mills?

Bring me my Bow of burning gold!
Bring me my Arrows of desire!
Bring me my Spear! O clouds, unfold!
Bring me my Chariot of fire!

I will not cease from Mental Fight,
Nor shall my Sword sleep in my hand,
Till we have built Jerusalem
In England's green and pleasant land.

Edmund Spenser (c. 1552–1599)

Prothalamion [extract]

The Crown still legally owns all the unmarked swans in British waters. 'Swan Upping' – in which teams of boatmen compete with the Queen's Swan Marker to save swans from the royal table by tagging them – still takes place on the Thames, although it now functions as a population census rather than a prelude to a tasty feast.

With that, I saw two swans of goodly hue
Come softly swimming down along the Lee;
Two fairer birds I yet did never see.
The snow which doth the top of Pindus strew,
Did never whiter shew,
Nor Jove himself, when he a swan would be
For love of Leda, whiter did appear:
Yet Leda was they say as white as he,
Yet not so white as these, nor nothing near.
So purely white they were,
That even the gentle stream, the which them bare,
Seemed foul to them, and bade his billows spare
To wet their silken feathers, lest they might
Soil their fair plumes with water not so fair,
And mar their beauties bright,
That shone as heaven's light,
Against their bridal day, which was not long:
      Sweet Thames, run softly, till I end my song.

William Shakespeare (1564–1616)

John of Gaunt's speech from Act II of *Richard II*

This royall Throne of Kings, this sceptred Isle,
This earth of Majesty, this seate of Mars,
This other Eden, demi-paradise,
This Fortresse built by Nature for her selfe
Against infection and the hand of warre,
This happy breed of men, this little world,
This precious stone set in the silver sea,
Which serves it in the office of a wall,
Or as a Moate defensive to a house,
Against the envy of lesse happier Lands,
This blessèd plot, this earth, this Realm, this England . . .

Vita Sackville-West (1892–1962)

The Land [extract]

The great estates of Knole, her childhood home, and Sissinghurst, where she created the famous gardens, are touchstones in Sackville-West's work. Her novel The Edwardians *and her lover Virginia Woolf's* Orlando *both celebrate the Kentish countryside around Knole in Sevenoaks.*

So the lush Weald to-day
Lies green in distance, and the horizon's sweep
Deepens to blue in woods, with the pointed spire
Pricking the foreground by the village tiles,
And the hop-kiln's whitened chimney stares between
Paler and darker green of Kentish miles,

And rarely a patch of corn in metal fire
Burnished by sunset ruffles in the green;
But meadow, shaw, and orchard keep
The glaucous country like a hilly sea
Pure in its monotone. Sad eyes that tire
Of dangerous landscape, sadder minds
That search impossible regions of their quest,
Find clement haven after truancy,
A temperate answer, and a makeshift rest.

Alexander Pope (1688–1744)

Ode on Solitude

*The acid-tongued bard of fashionable London sought tranquility in
the grounds of his residence in Twickenham, then something
of a rural backwater.*

Happy the man, whose wish and care
A few paternal acres bound,
Content to breathe his native air,
In his own ground.

Whose herds with milk, whose fields with bread,
Whose flocks supply him with attire,
Whose trees in summer yield him shade,
In winter fire.

Blest! who can unconcern'dly find
Hours, days, and years slide soft away,
In health of body, peace of mind,

Quiet by day,
Sound sleep by night; study and ease
Together mix'd; sweet recreation,
And innocence, which most does please,
With meditation.

Thus let me live, unseen, unknown;
Thus unlamented let me die;
Steal from the world, and not a stone
Tell where I lie.

Oliver Goldsmith (1730–1774)

The Deserted Village [extract]

Sweet Auburn! loveliest village of the plain,
Where health and plenty cheered the labouring swain,
Where smiling spring its earliest visit paid,
And parting summer's lingering blooms delayed:
Dear lovely bowers of innocence and ease,
Seats of my youth, when every sport could please,
How often have I loitered o'er thy green,
Where humble happiness endeared each scene;
How often have I paused on every charm,
The sheltered cot, the cultivated farm,
The never-failing brook, the busy mill,
The decent church that topped the neighbouring hill,
The hawthorn bush, with seats beneath the shade,
For talking age and whisp'ring lovers made;
How often have I blessed the coming day,
When toil remitting lent its turn to play,

And all the village train, from labour free,
Led up their sports beneath the spreading tree,
While many a pastime circled in the shade,
The young contending as the old surveyed;
And many a gambol frolicked o'er the ground,
And sleights of art and feats of strength went round;
And still as each repeated pleasure tired,
Succeeding sports the mirthful band inspired;
The dancing pair that simply sought renown,
By holding out to tire each other down;
The swain mistrustless of his smutted face,
While secret laughter tittered round the place;
The bashful virgin's sidelong looks of love,
The matron's glance that would those looks reprove:
These were thy charms, sweet village! sports like these,
With sweet succession, taught e'en toil to please;
These round thy bowers their cheerful influence shed,
These were thy charms – But all these charms are fled.

Gerard Manley Hopkins (1844–1889)

Pied Beauty

Hopkins was deeply religious and rather troubled, and he burned many of his early poems. Fortunately we still have a number of wonderful works by him, with their expressive sprung rhythm and inventive language. This is one of his finest.

Glory be to God for dappled things –
    For skies of couple-colour as a brinded cow;
        For rose-moles all in stipple upon trout that swim;

Fresh-firecoal chestnut-falls; finches' wings;
   Landscape plotted and pieced – fold, fallow, and plough;
     And áll trádes, their gear and tackle and trim.
All things counter, original, spare, strange;
   Whatever is fickle, freckled (who knows how?)
     With swift, slow; sweet, sour; adazzle, dim;
He fathers-forth whose beauty is past change:
               Praise him.

Ben Jonson (1572–1637)

To Penshurst

Rarely is the English countryside seen to better advantage than from the fine windows of a stately home. The country house poem proved an ideal way for seventeenth-century poets to praise the exquisite taste of their landed hosts and, presumably, ensure that they were invited again.

Thou art not, Penshurst, built to envious show,
Of touch or marble; nor canst boast a row
Of polish'd pillars, or a roof of gold;
Thou hast no lantern, whereof tales are told,
Or stair, or courts; but stand'st an ancient pile,
And, these grudged at, art reverenced the while.
Thou joy'st in better marks, of soil, of air,
Of wood, of water; therein thou art fair.
Thou hast thy walks for health, as well as sport;
Thy mount, to which the Dryads do resort,
Where Pan and Bacchus their high feasts have made,
Beneath the broad beach and the chestnut shade;
That taller tree, which of a nut was set

At his great birth, where all the Muses met.
There in the writhèd bark are cut the names
Of many a sylvan, taken with his flames;
And thence the ruddy Satyrs oft provoke
The lighter Fauns to reach thy Lady's Oak.
Thy copse too, named of Gamage, thou hast there,
That never fails to serve thee seasoned deer
When thou wouldst feast or exercise thy friends.
The lower land, that to the river bends,
Thy sheep, thy bullocks, kine, and calves do feed;
The middle grounds thy mares and horses breed.
Each bank doth yield thee conies; and the tops,
Fertile of wood, Ashore and Sidney's copse,
To crown thy open table, doth provide
The purple pheasant with the speckled side;
The painted partridge lies in every field,
And for thy mess is willing to be killed.
And if the high-swollen Medway fail thy dish,
Thou hast thy ponds, that pay thee tribute fish,
Fat aged carps that run into thy net,
And pikes, now weary their own kind to eat,
As loath the second draught or cast to stay,
Officiously at first themselves betray;
Bright eels that emulate them, and leap on land,
Before the fisher, or into his hand.
Then hath thy orchard fruit, thy garden flowers,
Fresh as the air, and new as are the hours.
The early cherry, with the later plum,
Fig, grape, and quince, each in his time doth come;
The blushing apricot and woolly peach
Hang on thy walls, that every child may reach.

A.A. Milne (1882–1956)

The Charcoal Burner

The Charcoal Burner has tales to tell.
He lives in the forest,
Alone in the forest;
He sits in the forest,
Alone in the forest.
When the sun comes slanting between the trees,
And rabbits come up, and they give him good morning,
And rabbits come up and say, 'beautiful morning' ...
When the moon swings clear of the tall black trees
And owls fly over and wish him goodnight,
Quietly over to wish him goodnight ...

And he sits and thinks of the things they know,
He and the forest, alone together –
The springs that come and the summers that go,
Autumn dew on bracken and heather,
The drip of the forest beneath the snow ...

All the things they have seen,
All the things they have heard:
An April sky swept clean and the song of a bird ...
Oh, the Charcoal Burner has tales to tell!
And he lives in the forest and knows us well.

Thomas Hardy (1840–1928)

In Time of 'The Breaking of Nations'

This contemplative poem celebrating the continuity of British rural life in the face of history's tempests was written in 1915, as the First World War ravaged the continent.

Only a man harrowing clods
    In a slow silent walk
With an old horse that stumbles and nods
    Half asleep as they stalk.

Only thin smoke without flame
    From the heaps of couch-grass;
Yet this will go onward the same
    Though Dynasties pass.

Yonder a maid and her wight
    Come whispering by:
War's annals will cloud into night
    Ere their story die.

Rudyard Kipling (1865–1936)

The Glory of the Garden

Our England is a garden that is full of stately views,
Of borders, beds and shrubberies and lawns and avenues,
With statues on the terraces and peacocks strutting by;
But the Glory of the Garden lies in more than meets the eye.

For where the thick laurels grow, along the thin red wall,
You will find the tool- and potting-sheds which are the heart of
    all;
The cold-frames and the hot-houses, the dungpits and the tanks,
The rollers, carts and drain-pipes, with the barrows and the
    planks.

And there you'll see the gardeners, the men and 'prentice boys
Told off to do as they are bid and do it without noise;
For, except when seeds are planted and we shout to scare the
    birds,
The Glory of the Garden it abideth not in words.

And some can pot begonias and some can bud a rose,
And some are hardly fit to trust with anything that grows;
But they can roll and trim the lawns and sift the sand and loam,
For the Glory of the Garden occupieth all who come.

Our England is a garden, and such gardens are not made
By singing:– 'Oh, how beautiful!' and sitting in the shade,
While better men than we go out and start their working lives
At grubbing weeds from gravel-paths with broken dinner-knives.

There's not a pair of legs so thin, there's not a head so thick,
There's not a hand so weak and white, nor yet a heart so sick,
But it can find some needful job that's crying to be done,
For the Glory of the Garden glorifieth every one.

Then seek your job with thankfulness and work till further
    orders,
If it's only netting strawberries or killing slugs on borders;

And when your back stops aching and your hands begin to
    harden,
You will find yourself a partner in the Glory of the Garden.

Oh, Adam was a gardener, and God who made him sees
That half a proper gardener's work is done upon his knees,
So when your work is finished, you can wash your hands
    and pray
For the Glory of the Garden, that it may not pass away!
And the Glory of the Garden it shall never pass away!

A.E. Housman (1859–1936)

XL. Into my heart an air that kills

The poems in Housman's popular pastoral volume, A Shropshire Lad, *were largely composed in London, showing how those marooned in the city can come to pine for country air.*

Into my heart an air that kills
  From yon far country blows:
What are those blue remembered hills,
  What spires, what farms are those?

That is the land of lost content,
  I see it shining plain,
The happy highways where I went
  And cannot come again.

Rupert Brooke (1887–1915)

The Soldier

It was a certain England for which Brooke and so many of his contemporaries were prepared to die: a rural England found out of doors in the shires and wolds, where young men sunned themselves in a pre-war idyll that endured only in wistful poems that emerged from the trenches.

If I should die, think only this of me:
    That there's some corner of a foreign field
That is for ever England. There shall be
    In that rich earth a richer dust concealed;
A dust whom England bore, shaped, made aware,
    Gave, once, her flowers to love, her ways to roam,
A body of England's, breathing English air,
    Washed by the rivers, blest by suns of home.

And think, this heart, all evil shed away,
    A pulse in the eternal mind, no less
        Gives somewhere back the thoughts by England given;
Her sights and sounds; dreams happy as her day;
    And laughter, learnt of friends; and gentleness,
        In hearts at peace, under an English heaven.

SPRING

No season excites poets as much as spring, when the world wakes from wintry slumber, inspiring pleasure and thoughts of resurrection. It seems in some ways the most British of seasons, perhaps because it is often typified by frequent rain showers. In this selection, Swinburne and Shelley pine for the green beauties of spring while in the grasp of winter, and Lee, Chaucer and Browning all evoke the pleasures of the short month of April.

Robert Browning (1812–1889)

Home-Thoughts, from Abroad

Browning eloped to Italy with his wife, Elizabeth Barrett Browning, and this much-loved poem expresses the expatriate's nostalgia so beautifully captured in its title.

Oh, to be in England
Now that April's there,
And whoever wakes in England
Sees, some morning, unaware,
That the lowest boughs and the brushwood sheaf
Round the elm-tree bole are in tiny leaf,
While the chaffinch sings on the orchard bough
In England – now!

And after April, when May follows,
And the whitethroat builds, and all the swallows!
Hark, where my blossomed pear-tree in the hedge
Leans to the field and scatters on the clover
Blossoms and dewdrops – at the bent spray's edge –
That's the wise thrush; he sings each song twice over,
Lest you should think he never could recapture
The first fine careless rapture!
And though the fields look rough with hoary dew
All will be gay when noontide wakes anew
The buttercups, the little children's dower
– Far brighter than this gaudy melon-flower!

Geoffrey Chaucer (c.1343–1400)

The Canterbury Tales [General Prologue]

Whan that April with his showres soote
The droughte of March hath perced to the roote,
And bathed every veine in swich licour,
Of which vertu engendred is the flowr;
Whan Zephyrus eek with his sweete breeth
Inspired hath in every holt and heeth
The tendre croppes, and the yonge sonne
Hath in the Ram his halve cours yronne,
And smale fowles maken melodye
That sleepen al the night with open yë –
So priketh hem Nature in hir corages –
Thanne longen folk to goon on pilgrimages,
And palmeres for to seeken straunge strondes
To ferne halwes, couthe in sondry londes;
And specially from every shires ende
Of Engelond to Canterbury they wende,
The holy blisful martyr for to seeke
That hem hath holpen whan that they were seke.

(*His* – its; *soote* – fresh; *swich* – such; *licour* – liquid; *Zephyrus* – the West Wind; *eek* – also; *inspired* – breathed into; *holt* – grove; *heeth* – field; *croppes* – shoots; *'Hath . . . yronne'* – the 'young' sun is only halfway through its course in Aries (the first sign of the zodiac, which the sun enters at the vernal equinox, 20 March); *fowles* – birds; *yë* – eye; *hem* – them; *hir corages* – their hearts; *goon* – go; *palmeres* – palmers (far-travelling pilgrims); *ferne* – faraway; *halwes* – shrines; *couthe* – known; *londes* – lands; *holpen* – helped; *seke* – sick.)

Algernon Charles Swinburne (1837–1909)

A Vision of Spring in Winter [extract]

The London-born Swinburne considered himself to be Northumbrian, having spent summers at his grandfather's country seat, Capheaton Hall. He enjoyed a healthy, outdoorsy childhood swimming and riding there and on the Isle of Wight, though he led a rather more decadent adult life.

O tender time that love thinks long to see,
    Sweet foot of spring that with her footfall sows
    Late snowlike flowery leavings of the snows,
Be not too long irresolute to be;
O mother-month, where have they hidden thee?
    Out of the pale time of the flowerless rose
I reach my heart out toward the springtime lands,
    I stretch my spirit forth to the fair hours,
        The purplest of the prime:
I lean my soul down over them, with hands
    Made wide to take the ghostly growths of flowers:
        I send my love back to the lovely time.

Where has the greenwood hid thy gracious head?
    Veiled with what visions while the grey world grieves,
    Or muffled with what shadows of green leaves,
What warm intangible green shadows spread
To sweeten the sweet twilight for thy bed?
    What sleep enchants thee? what delight deceives?
Where the deep dreamlike dew before the dawn
    Feels not the fingers of the sunlight yet
        Its silver web unweave,

Thy footless ghost on some unfooted lawn
    Whose air the unrisen sunbeams fear to fret
        Lives a ghost's life of daylong dawn and eve.

Thomas Nashe (1567–1601)

Spring, the Sweet Spring. From *Summer's Last Will and Testament*

Summer's Last Will and Testament was originally written to be performed as an Elizabethan masque. Nashe, by birth a Suffolk boy, was staying in the then rural area of Croydon when he wrote it.

Spring, the sweet spring, is the year's pleasant king,
Then blooms each thing, then maids dance in a ring,
Cold doth not sting, the pretty birds do sing:
    Cuckoo, jug-jug, pu-we, to-witta-woo!

The palm and may make country houses gay,
Lambs frisk and play, the shepherds pipe all day,
And we hear aye birds tune this merry lay:
    Cuckoo, jug-jug, pu-we, to-witta-woo!

The fields breathe sweet, the daisies kiss our feet,
Young lovers meet, old wives a-sunning sit,
In every street these tunes our ears do greet:
    Cuckoo, jug-jug, pu-we, to-witta-woo!
      Spring, the sweet spring!

Percy Bysshe Shelley (1792–1822)

The Question

I dreamed that, as I wandered by the way,
    Bare Winter suddenly was changed to Spring,
And gentle odours led my steps astray,
    Mixed with a sound of waters murmuring
Along a shelving bank of turf, which lay
    Under a copse, and hardly dared to fling
Its green arms round the bosom of the stream,
But kissed it and then fled, as thou mightest in dream.

There grew pied wind-flowers and violets,
    Daisies, those pearled Arcturi of the earth,
The constellated flower that never sets;
    Faint oxlips; tender bluebells, at whose birth
The sod scarce heaved; and that tall flower that wets—
    Like a child, half in tenderness and mirth—
Its mother's face with Heaven's collected tears,
When the low wind, its playmate's voice, it hears.

And in the warm hedge grew lush eglantine,
    Green cowbind and the moonlight-coloured may,
And cherry-blossoms, and white cups, whose wine
    Was the bright dew, yet drained not by the day;
And wild roses, and ivy serpentine,
    With its dark buds and leaves, wandering astray;
And flowers azure, black, and streaked with gold,
Fairer than any wakened eyes behold.

And nearer to the river's trembling edge
    There grew broad flag-flowers, purple pranked with white,
And starry river buds among the sedge,
    And floating water-lilies, broad and bright,
Which lit the oak that overhung the hedge
    With moonlight beams of their own watery light;
And bulrushes, and reeds of such deep green
As soothed the dazzled eye with sober sheen.

Methought that of these visionary flowers
    I made a nosegay, bound in such a way
That the same hues, which in their natural bowers
    Were mingled or opposed, the like array
Kept these imprisoned children of the Hours
    Within my hand,—and then, elate and gay,
I hastened to the spot whence I had come,
That I might there present it!—Oh! to whom?

Laurie Lee (1914–1997)

April Rise

If ever I saw blessing in the air
    I see it now in this still early day
Where lemon-green the vaporous morning drips
    Wet sunlight on the powder of my eye.

Blown bubble-film of blue, the sky wraps round
    Weeds of warm light whose every root and rod
Splutters with soapy green, and all the world
    Sweats with the bead of summer in its bud.

If ever I heard blessing it is there
    Where birds in trees that shoals and shadows are
Splash with their hidden wings and drops of sound
    Break on my ears their crests of throbbing air.

Pure in the haze the emerald sun dilates,
    The lips of sparrows milk the mossy stones,
While white as water by the lake a girl
    Swims her green hand among the gathered swans.

Now, as the almond burns its smoking wick,
    Dropping small flames to light the candled grass;
Now, as my low blood scales its second chance,
    If ever world were blessed, now it is.

Christopher Marlowe (1564–1593)

The Passionate Shepherd to His Love

*Marlowe was hardly a country lad, since he was born in Canterbury,
educated at Cambridge and spent his often controversial career in
London, so this sweet pastoral verse is unusual in his work.*

Come live with me and be my love,
And we will all the pleasures prove,
That hills and valleys, dales and fields,
And all the craggy mountains yields.

There we will sit upon the rocks,
And see the shepherds feed their flocks,
By shallow rivers to whose falls
Melodious birds sing madrigals.

And I will make thee beds of roses
And a thousand fragrant posies,
A cap of flowers, and a kirtle
Embroider'd all with leaves of myrtle.

A gown made of the finest wool
Which from our pretty lambs we pull;
Fair linèd slippers for the cold,
With buckles of the purest gold.

A belt of straw and ivy buds,
With coral clasps and amber studs:
And if these pleasures may thee move,
Come live with me and be my love.
Thy silver dishes for thy meat

As precious as the gods do eat,
Shall on an ivory table be
Prepared each day for thee and me.

The shepherds' swains shall dance and sing
For thy delight each May morning:
If these delights thy mind may move,
Then live with me and be my love.

Elizabeth Barrett Browning (1806–1861)

Aurora Leigh [extract]

But then the thrushes sang,
And shook my pulses and the elms' new leaves ...
I flattered all the beauteous country round,
As poets use; the skies, the clouds, the fields,
The happy violets hiding from the roads
The primroses run down to, carrying gold, –
The tangled hedgerows, where the cows push out
Impatient horns and tolerant churning mouths
'Twixt dripping ash-boughs, – hedgerows all alive
With birds and gnats and large white butterflies
Which look as if the May-flower had caught life
And palpitated forth upon the wind, –
Hills, vales, woods, netted in a silver mist,
Farms, granges, doubled up among the hills,
And cattle grazing in the watered vales,
And cottage-chimneys smoking from the woods,
And cottage-gardens smelling everywhere,
Confused with smell of orchards.

John Milton (1608–1674)

Paradise Lost [extract]

Although Milton was well travelled within Europe for a man of his time, and despite all the grapes and aromatic gum trees, it is easy to see England in this Eden with its sheep-studded lawns and valleys.

Thus was this place,
A happy rural seat of various view:
Groves whose rich trees wept odorous gums and balm,
Others whose fruit, burnished with golden rind,
Hung amiable – Hesperian fables true,
If true, here only – and of delicious taste.
Betwixt them lawns, or level downs, and flocks
Grazing the tender herb, were interposed,
Or palmy hillock; or the flowery lap
Of some irriguous valley spread her store,
Flowers of all hue, and without thorn the rose.
Another side, umbrageous grots and caves
Of cool recess, o'er which the mantling vine
Lays forth her purple grape, and gently creeps
Luxuriant; meanwhile murmuring waters fall
Down the slope hills, dispersed, or in a lake,
That to the fringed bank with myrtle crowned,
Her crystal mirror holds, unite their streams.
The birds their quire apply; airs, vernal airs,
Breathing the smell of field and grove, attune
The trembling leaves, while universal Pan,
Knit with the Graces and the Hours in dance,
Led on the eternal Spring.

William Shakespeare (1564–1616)

Spring. From *Love's Labour Lost*

When daisies pied and violets blue
   And lady-smocks all silver-white
And cuckoo-buds of yellow hue
   Do paint the meadows with delight,
The cuckoo then, on every tree,
Mocks married men; for thus sings he,
               Cuckoo!
Cuckoo, cuckoo! O, word of fear,
Unpleasing to a married ear!

When shepherds pipe on oaten straws,
   And merry larks are ploughmen's clocks,
When turtles tread, and rooks, and daws,
   And maidens bleach their summer smocks,
The cuckoo then, on every tree,
Mocks married men; for thus sings he,
               Cuckoo!
Cuckoo, cuckoo! O, word of fear,
Unpleasing to a married ear!

Alfred, Lord Tennyson

The Lady of Shalott [extract]

On either side the river lie
Long fields of barley and of rye,
That clothe the wold and meet the sky;
And thro' the field the road runs by
To many-towered Camelot;
And up and down the people go,
Gazing where the lilies blow
Round an island there below,

The island of Shalott.
Willows whiten, aspens quiver,
Little breezes dusk and shiver
Thro' the wave that runs for ever
By the island in the river
Flowing down to Camelot.
Four grey walls, and four grey towers,
Overlook a space of flowers,
And the silent isle imbowers
The Lady of Shalott.

Gerard Manley Hopkins (1844–1889)

Spring

Nothing is so beautiful as Spring –
    When weeds, in wheels, shoot long and lovely and lush;
    Thrush's eggs look little low heavens, and thrush
Through the echoing timber does so rinse and wring
The ear, it strikes like lightnings to hear him sing;
    The glassy peartree leaves and blooms, they brush
    The descending blue; that blue is all in a rush
With richness; the racing lambs too have fair their fling.

What is all this juice and all this joy?
    A strain of the earth's sweet being in the beginning
In Eden garden. – Have, get, before it cloy,

    Before it cloud, Christ, lord, and sour with sinning,
Innocent mind and Mayday in girl and boy,
    Most, O maid's child, thy choice and worthy the winning.

Robert Herrick (1591–1674)

Corinna's Going a-Maying

*Herrick spent much of his career as a vicar in Devon, and his verses
reflect the rhythms of rural life. He was said to have a pet pig that he
had trained to drink from a tankard.*

Get up, get up for shame, the Blooming Morne
Upon her wings presents the god unshorne.

See how Aurora throwes her faire
Fresh-quilted colours through the aire:
   Get up, sweet-Slug-a-bed, and see
   The Dew-bespangling Herbe and Tree.
Each Flower has wept, and bow'd toward the East,
Above an houre since; yet you not drest,
   Nay! not so much as out of bed?
   When all the Birds have Matins seyd,
   And sung their thankful Hymnes: 'tis sin,
   Nay, profanation to keep in,
When as a thousand Virgins on this day,
Spring, sooner than the Lark, to fetch in May.

Rise; and put on your Foliage, and be seene
To come forth, like the Spring-time, fresh and greene;
   And sweet as Flora. Take no care
   For Jewels for your Gowne, or Haire:
   Feare not; the leaves will strew
   Gemms in abundance upon you:
Besides, the childhood of the Day has kept,
Against you come, some Orient Pearls unwept:
   Come, and receive them while the light
   Hangs on the Dew-locks of the night:
   And Titan on the Eastern hill
   Retires himselfe, or else stands still
Till you come forth. Wash, dresse, be briefe in praying:
Few Beads are best, when once we goe a Maying.

Come, my Corinna, come; and comming, marke
How each field turns a street; each street a Parke
   Made green, and trimm'd with trees: see how
   Devotion gives each House a Bough,
   Or Branch: Each Porch, each doore, ere this,

An Arke a Tabernacle is
Made up of white-thorn neatly enterwove;
As if here were those cooler shades of love.
    Can such delights be in the street,
    And open fields, and we not see't?
    Come, we'll abroad; and let's obay
    The Proclamation made for May:
And sin no more, as we have done, by staying;
But my Corinna, come, let's goe a Maying.

There's not a budding Boy, or Girle, this day,
But is got up, and gone to bring in May.
    A deale of Youth, ere this, is come
    Back, and with White-thorn laden home.
    Some have dispatcht their Cakes and Creame,
    Before that we have left to dreame:
And some have wept, and woo'd, and plighted Troth,
And chose their Priest, ere we can cast off sloth:
    Many a green-gown has been given;
    Many a kisse, both odde and even:
    Many a glance too has been sent
    From out the eye, Loves Firmament:
Many a jest told of the Keyes betraying
This night, and Locks pickt, yet w'are not a Maying.
Come, let us goe, while we are in our prime;
And take the harmlesse follie of the time.
    We shall grow old apace, and die
    Before we know our liberty.
    Our life is short; and our dayes run
    As fast away as do's the Sunne:
And as a vapour, or a drop of raine
Once lost, can ne'r be found againe:
    So when or you or I are made

A fable, song, or fleeting shade;
All love, all liking, all delight
Lies drown'd with us in endlesse night.
Then while time serves, and we are but decaying;
Come, my Corinna, come, let's goe a Maying.

William Wordsworth (1770–1850)

I Wandered Lonely as a Cloud

The excitement of that first glimpse of bright daffodils after a long winter has never been better expressed.

I wandered lonely as a cloud
That floats on high o'er vales and hills,
When all at once I saw a crowd,
A host, of golden daffodils;
Beside the lake, beneath the trees,
Fluttering and dancing in the breeze.
Continuous as the stars that shine
And twinkle on the milky way,
They stretched in never-ending line
Along the margin of a bay:
Ten thousand saw I at a glance,
Tossing their heads in sprightly dance.

The waves beside them danced; but they
Outdid the sparkling waves in glee;
A poet could not but be gay,
In such a jocund company:

I gazed – and gazed – but little thought
What wealth the show to me had brought:

For oft, when on my couch I lie
In vacant or in pensive mood,
They flash upon that inward eye
Which is the bliss of solitude;
And then my heart with pleasure fills,
And dances with the daffodils.

Charlotte Mew (1869–1928)

I so liked Spring

Mew is not well known now, though she won praise from contemporaries including Thomas Hardy, Virginia Woolf and Siegfried Sassoon.

I so liked Spring last year
        Because you were here;–
                The thrushes too–
Because it was these you so liked to hear–
                I so liked you.

        This year's a different thing,–
                I'll not think of you.
But I'll like Spring because it is simply Spring
                As the thrushes do.

Birds

If you have heard birds trilling on a spring morning, calling to each other from the corners of a wood, carolling at early winter twilight, or drowsily cooing on a hot afternoon, you will understand at once why so many poets have chosen to write about British birds. Birdwatching in the countryside is, like composing poetry, an activity pursued most easily in solitude.

John Clare (1793–1864)

Autumn Birds

Clare was from a farming background and, unlike so many grander men singing the praises of hardworking rural folk, composed his poems with his hands literally in the soil.

The wild duck startles like a sudden thought,
And heron slow as if it might be caught.
The flopping crows on weary wings go by
And grey beard jackdaws noising as they fly.
The crowds of starnels whizz and hurry by,
And darken like a cloud the evening sky.
The larks like thunder rise and suthy round,
Then drop and nestle in the stubble ground.
The wild swan hurries hight and noises loud
With white neck peering to the evening cloud.
The weary rooks to distant woods are gone.
With lengths of tail the magpie winnows on
To neighbouring tree, and leaves the distant crow
While small birds nestle in the hedge below.

Gerard Manley Hopkins (1844–1889)

The Windhover

I caught this morning morning's minion, king-
    dom of daylight's dauphin, dapple-dawn-drawn Falcon, in
      his riding
    Of the rolling level underneath him steady air, and striding
High there, how he rung upon the rein of a wimpling wing
In his ecstasy! then off, off forth on swing,
    As a skate's heel sweeps smooth on a bow-bend: the hurl
      and gliding
    Rebuffed the big wind. My heart in hiding
Stirred for a bird, – the achieve of, the mastery of the thing!

Brute beauty and valour and act, oh, air, pride, plume, here
    Buckle! And the fire that breaks from thee then, a billion
Times told lovelier, more dangerous, O my chevalier!

    No wonder of it: shéer plód makes plough down sillion
Shine, and blue-bleak embers, ah my dear,
    Fall, gall themselves, and gash gold-vermilion.

Ted Hughes (1930–1998)

Hawk Roosting

Hughes was greatly inspired by an unsentimental vision of the English countryside, especially the rugged landscape of Yorkshire where his childhood was spent.

I sit in the top of the wood, my eyes closed.
Inaction, no falsifying dream
Between my hooked head and hooked feet:
Or in sleep rehearse perfect kills and eat.

The convenience of the high trees!
The air's buoyancy and the sun's ray
Are of advantage to me;
And the earth's face upward for my inspection.

My feet are locked upon the rough bark.
It took the whole of Creation
To produce my foot, my each feather:
Now I hold Creation in my foot

Or fly up, and revolve it all slowly -
I kill where I please because it is all mine.
There is no sophistry in my body:
My manners are tearing off heads -

The allotment of death.
For the one path of my flight is direct
Through the bones of the living.
No arguments assert my right:

The sun is behind me.
Nothing has changed since I began.
My eye has permitted no change.
I am going to keep things like this.

W. H. Davies (1871–1940)

The Kingfisher

It was the Rainbow gave thee birth,
   And left thee all her lovely hues;
And, as her mother's name was Tears,
   So runs it in thy blood to choose
For haunts the lonely pools, and keep
In company with trees that weep.

Go you and, with such glorious hues,
   Live with proud peacocks in green parks;
On lawns as smooth as shining glass,
   Let every feather show its marks;
Get thee on boughs and clap thy wings
Before the windows of proud kings.

Nay, lovely Bird, thou art not vain;
   Thou hast no proud, ambitious mind;
I also love a quiet place
   That's green, away from all mankind;
A lonely pool, and let a tree
Sigh with her bosom over me.

Percy Bysshe Shelley (1792–1822)

To a Skylark [extracts]

Although he famously spent his later years in Italy, Shelley was born in Sussex and lived for a time in the Lake District. His poetry often evokes the beauties of the English countryside.

Hail to thee, blithe Spirit!
    Bird thou never wert,
That from Heaven, or near it,
    Pourest thy full heart
In profuse strains of unpremeditated art.

Higher still and higher
    From the earth thou springest
Like a cloud of fire;
    The blue deep thou wingest,
And singing still dost soar, and soaring ever singest.

In the golden light'ning
    Of the sunken sun,
O'er which clouds are bright'ning,
    Thou dost float and run,
Like an unbodied joy whose race is just begun.

The pale purple even
    Melts around thy flight;
Like a star of Heaven,
    In the broad daylight
Thou art unseen, but yet I hear thy shrill delight,

Teach me half the gladness
    That thy brain must know,
Such harmonious madness
    From my lips would flow
The world should listen then – as I am listening now.

Anonymous

Who Killed Cock Robin?

Who killed Cock Robin?
'I,' said the Sparrow,
'With my bow and arrow,
I killed Cock Robin.'

Who saw him die?
'I,' said the Fly,
'With my little eye,
I saw him die.'

Who'll dig his grave?
'I,' said the Owl,
'With my spade and trowel,
I'll dig his grave.'

Who'll be the parson?
'I,' said the Rook,
'With my little book,
I'll be the parson.'

Who'll be chief mourner?
'I,' said the Dove,
'For I mourn my love,
I'll be chief mourner.'

Who'll sing a psalm?
'I,' said the Thrush,
As she sat on a bush.
'I'll sing a psalm.'

Who'll carry the coffin?
'I,' said the Kite,
'If it's not through the night,
I'll carry the coffin.'

Who'll toll the bell?
'I,' said the Bull,
'Because I can pull,
I'll toll the bell.'

All the birds of the air
Fell a-sighing and a-sobbing,
When they heard the bell toll
For poor Cock Robin.

Morning

As the countryside shakes off the night and the day begins, everything seems possible. The solitude of the early hours, the sounds of the dawn chorus and the beauty of the land in the morning light have inspired some of the most delightful verses in the English language.

John Clare (1793–1864)

On a Lane in Spring

A Little Lane, the brook runs close beside,
    And spangles in the sunshine while the fish glide swiftly by;
And hedges leafing with the green spring tide;
    From out their greenery the old birds fly,
And chirp and whistle in the morning sun;
    The pilewort glitters 'neath the pale blue sky,
The little robin has its nest begun
    The grass-green linnets round the bushes fly.
How Mild the Spring Comes in; the daisy buds
    Lift up their golden blossoms to the sky.
How lovely are the pingles in the woods!
    Here a beetle runs; and there a fly
Rests on the Arum leaf in bottle-green
    And all the Spring in this Sweet lane is seen.

Andrew Marvell (1621–1678)

Upon Appleton House [extract]

Marvell stayed at Nun Appleton, the Yorkshire estate of Thomas, Lord Fairfax, while serving as tutor to his daughter. Upon Appleton House *examines the merits of rural retirement, ascribing many of the house's pleasant qualities to its master.*

When in the east the morning ray
Hangs out the colours of the day,
The bee through these known alleys hums
Beating the dian with its drums.
Then flowers their drowsy eyelids raise,
Their silken ensigns each displays,
And dries its pan yet dank with dew,
And fills its flask with odours new.

A. E. Housman (1859–1936)

Spring Morning

Star and coronal and bell
   April underfoot renews,
And the hope of man as well
   Flowers among the morning dews.

Now the old come out to look,
   Winter past and winter's pains,
How the sky in pool and brook
   Glitters on the grassy plains.

Easily the gentle air
   Wafts the turning season on;
Things to comfort them are there,
   Though 'tis true the best are gone.

Now the scorned unlucky lad
   Rousing from his pillow gnawn
Mans his heart and deep and glad
   Drinks the valiant air of dawn.

Half the night he longed to die,
   Now are sown on hill and plain
Pleasures worth his while to try
   Ere he longs to die again.

Blue the sky from east to west
   Arches, and the world is wide,
Though the girl he loves the best
   Rouses from another's side.

Alfred, Lord Tennyson (1809–1892)

In Memoriam [extract]

Tennyson's epic elegy for his beloved friend Arthur Henry Hallam
includes the famous lines concerning 'nature red in tooth and claw', but
this section has a gentler and happier atmosphere.

Calm is the morn without a sound,
   Calm as to suit a calmer grief,
   And only through the faded leaf
The chestnut pattering to the ground:

Calm and deep peace on this high wold,
   And on these dews that drench the furze,
   And all the silvery gossamers
That twinkle into green and gold:

Calm and still light on yon great plain
   That sweeps with all its autumn bowers,
   And crowded farms and lessening towers,
To mingle with the bounding main:

Calm and deep peace in this wide air,
   These leaves that redden to the fall;
   And in my heart, if calm at all,
If any calm, a calm despair:

Calm on the seas, and silver sleep,
   And waves that sway themselves in rest,
   And dead calm in the noble breast
Which heaves but with the heaving deep.

Edward Thomas (1878–1917)

The Glory

The glory of the beauty of the morning, –
The cuckoo crying over the untouched dew;
The blackbird that has found it, and the dove
That tempts me on to something sweeter than love;
White clouds ranged even and fair as new-mown hay;
The heat, the stir, the sublime vacancy
Of sky and meadow and forest and my own heart: –
The glory invites me, yet it leaves me scorning
All I can ever do, all I can be,
Beside the lovely of motion, shape, and hue,
The happiness I fancy fit to dwell
In beauty's presence. Shall I now this day
Begin to seek as far as heaven, as hell,
Wisdom or strength to match this beauty, start
And tread the pale dust pitted with small dark drops,
In hope to find whatever it is I seek,
Hearkening to short-lived happy-seeming things
That we know naught of, in the hazel copse?
Or must I be content with discontent
As larks and swallows are perhaps with wings?
And shall I ask at the day's end once more
What beauty is, and what I can have meant
By happiness? And shall I let all go,
Glad, weary, or both? Or shall I perhaps know
That I was happy oft and oft before,
Awhile forgetting how I am fast pent,
How dreary-swift, with naught to travel to,
Is Time? I cannot bite the day to the core.

Trees

Britain has always been, and is still, a wooded land. William the Conqueror's Forest Law placed woodlands under royal ownership for the first time, but they have been seen as both places of refuge and menace for ordinary folk throughout the nation's history. Tales of legendary Merry Men, kings up trees and ghostly babes endure in the popular imagination, and the oak remains a potent symbol of the vigour and resilience of old England. Poets have written much about the contemplative delights of a wander through the woods.

A. E. Housman (1859–1936)

Loveliest of Trees, the Cherry Now

Loveliest of trees, the cherry now
Is hung with bloom along the bough,
And stands about the woodland ride
Wearing white for Eastertide.

Now, of my threescore years and ten,
Twenty will not come again,
And take from seventy springs a score,
It only leaves me fifty more.

And since to look at things in bloom
Fifty springs are little room,
About the woodlands I will go
To see the cherry hung with snow.

Philip Larkin (1922–1985)

The Trees

The trees are coming into leaf
Like something almost being said;
The recent buds relax and spread,
Their greenness is a kind of grief.

Is it that they are born again
And we grow old? No, they die too.
Their yearly trick of looking new
Is written down in rings of grain.

Yet still the unresting castles thresh
In fullgrown thickness every May.
Last year is dead, they seem to say,
Begin afresh, afresh, afresh.

Louis MacNeice (1907–1963)

Woods

Northern Irish MacNeice was educated in England and spent much of his life working for the BBC.

My father who found the English landscape tame
Had hardly in his life walked in a wood,
Too old when first he met one; Malory's knights,
Keats's nymphs or the Midsummer Night's Dream
Could never arras the room, where he spelled out True
    and Good
With their interleaving of half-truths and not-quites.

While for me from the age of ten the socketed wooden gate
Into a Dorset planting, into a dark
But gentle ambush, was an alluring eye;
Within was a kingdom free from time and sky,
Caterpillar webs on the forehead, danger under the feet,
And the mind adrift in a floating and rustling ark

Packed with birds and ghosts, two of every race,
Trills of love from the picture-book – Oh might I never land
But here, grown six foot tall, find me also a love
Also out of the picture-book; whose hand
Would be soft as the webs of the wood and on her face
The wood-pigeon's voice would shaft a chrism from above.

So in a grassy ride a rain-filled hoof-mark coined
By a finger of sun from the mint of Long Ago
Was the last of Lancelot's glitter. Make-believe dies hard;
That the rider passed here lately and is a man we know

Is still untrue, the gate to Legend remains unbarred,
The grown-up hates to divorce what the child joined.

Thus from a city when my father would frame
Escape, he thought, as I do, of bog or rock
But I have also this other, this English, choice
Into what yet is foreign; whatever its name
Each wood is the mystery and the recurring shock
Of its dark coolness is a foreign voice.

Yet in using the word tame my father was maybe right,
These woods are not the Forest; each is moored
To a village somewhere near. If not of today
They are not like the wilds of Mayo, they are assured
Of their place by men; reprieved from the neolithic night
By gamekeepers or by Herrick's girls at play.

And always we walk out again. The patch
Of sky at the end of the path grows and discloses
An ordered open air long ruled by dyke and fence,
With geese whose form and gait proclaim their consequence,
Pargetted outposts, windows browed with thatch,
And cow pats – and inconsequent wild roses.

Siegfried Sassoon (1886–1967)

Wind in the Beechwood

Sassoon is now best remembered for his bitter and satirical First World War poetry, but this meditation on a beechwood – a very British locale – finds him in gentler voice.

The glorying forest shakes and swings with glancing
Of boughs that dip and strain; young, slanting sprays
Beckon and shift like lissom creatures dancing,
While the blown beechwood streams with drifting rays.
   Rooted in steadfast calm, grey stems are seen
   Like weather-beaten masts; the wood, unfurled,
   Seems as a ship with crowding sails of green
   That sweeps across the lonely billowing world.

O luminous and lovely! Let your flowers,
Your ageless-squadroned wings, your surge and gleam,
Drown me in quivering brightness: let me fade
   In the warm, rustling music of the hours
   That guard your ancient wisdom, till my dream
   Moves with the chant and whisper of the glade.

Coventry Patmore (1823–1896)

Arbor Vitae

With honeysuckle, over-sweet, festoon'd;
With bitter ivy bound;
Terraced with funguses unsound;

Deform'd with many a boss
And closed scar, o'ercushion'd deep with moss;
Bunch'd all about with pagan mistletoe;
And thick with nests of the hoarse bird
That talks, but understands not his own word;
Stands, and so stood a thousand years ago,
A single tree.
Thunder has done its worst among its twigs,
Where the great crest yet blackens, never pruned,
But in its heart, alway
Ready to push new verdurous boughs, whene'er
The rotting saplings near it fall and leave it air,
Is all antiquity and no decay.
Rich, though rejected by the forest-pigs,
Its fruit, beneath whose rough, concealing rind
They that will break it find
Heart-succouring savour of each several meat,
And kernell'd drink of brain-renewing power,
With bitter condiment and sour,
And sweet economy of sweet,
And odours that remind
Of haunts of childhood and a different day.
Beside this tree,
Praising no Gods nor blaming, sans a wish,
Sits, Tartar-like, the Time's civility,
And eats its dead-dog off a golden dish.

Christina Rossetti (1830–1894)

The Trees' Counselling

I was strolling sorrowfully
    Thro' the corn fields and the meadows;
The stream sounded melancholy,
    And I walked among the shadows;
While the ancient forest trees
Talked together in the breeze;
In the breeze that waved and blew them,
With a strange weird rustle thro' them.

Said the oak unto the others
    In a leafy voice and pleasant:
'Here we all are equal brothers,
    'Here we have nor lord nor peasant.
'Summer, Autumn, Winter, Spring,
'Pass in happy following.
'Little winds may whistle by us,
'Little birds may overfly us;

'But the sun still waits in heaven
    'To look down on us in splendour;
'When he goes the moon is given,
    'Full of rays that he doth lend her:
'And tho' sometimes in the night
'Mists may hide her from our sight,
'She comes out in the calm weather,
'With the glorious stars together.'

From the fruitage, from the blossom,
    From the trees came no denying;
Then my heart said in my bosom:

'Wherefore art thou sad and sighing?
'Learn contentment from this wood
'That proclaimeth all states good;
'Go not from it as it found thee;
'Turn thyself and gaze around thee.'

And I turned: behold the shading
        But showed forth the light more clearly;
The wild bees were honey-lading;
        The stream sounded hushing merely,
And the wind not murmuring
Seemed, but gently whispering:
'Get thee patience; and thy spirit
'Shall discern in all things merit.'

Gerard Manley Hopkins (1844–1889)

Binsey Poplars

The lament for lost countryside has preoccupied British poets for centuries, and it seems that no tree is mourned more gravely than the poplar, if Cowper and Hopkins are to be believed.

My aspens dear, whose airy cages quelled,
Quelled or quenched in leaves the leaping sun,
All felled, felled, are all felled;
Of a fresh and following folded rank
Not spared, not one
That dandled a sandalled
Shadow that swam or sank
On meadow and river and wind-wandering weed-winding bank.

O if we but knew what we do
When we delve or hew –
Hack and rack the growing green!
Since country is so tender
To touch, her being so slender,
That, like this sleek and seeing ball
But a prick will make no eye at all,
Where we, even where we mean
To mend her we end her,
When we hew or delve:
After-comers cannot guess the beauty been.
Ten or twelve, only ten or twelve
Strokes of havoc unselve
The sweet especial scene,
Rural scene, a rural scene,
Sweet especial rural scene.

William Cowper (1731–1800)

The Poplar-Field

The poplars are felled, farewell to the shade
And the whispering sound of the cool colonnade,
The winds play no longer, and sing in the leaves,
Nor Ouse on his bosom their image receives.

Twelve years have elapsed since I last took a view
Of my favourite field and the bank where they grew,
And now in the grass behold they are laid,
And the tree is my seat that once lent me a shade.

The blackbird has fled to another retreat
Where the hazels afford him a screen from the heat,
And the scene where his melody charmed me before,
Resounds with his sweet-flowing ditty no more.

My fugitive years are all hasting away,
And I must ere long lie as lowly as they,
With a turf on my breast, and a stone at my head,
Ere another such grove shall arise in its stead.

'Tis a sight to engage me, if any thing can,
To muse on the perishing pleasures of man;
Though his life be a dream, his enjoyments, I see,
Have a being less durable even than he.

Summer

The British summertime is cruelly maligned, though each generation seems convinced that endless, balmy August days existed only during their own childhood. However, the unreliability of our summer weather imbues those drowsy golden days – when they are granted us – with a precious quality the inhabitants of warmer climes can never quite comprehend. Poets have understandably been moved to raptures by the perfumed loveliness of the British landscape under the sun.

Anonymous

Sumer is icumen in

Sumer is icumen in,
Lhude sing, cuccu!
Groweth sed and bloweth med
And springth the wude nu.
Sing, cuccu!

Awe bleteth after lomb,
Lhouth after calve cu,
Bulluc sterteth, bucke verteth.
Murie sing, cuccu!
Cuccu, cuccu,
Wel singes thu, cuccu!
Ne swik thu naver nu!

Sing, cuccu, nu! Sing, cuccu!
Sing, cuccu! Sing, cuccu nu!

(*Lhude* – loud; *sed* – seed; *med* – mead; *wude* – wood; *nu* – anew;
awe – ewe; *lomb* – lamb; *llouth* – lows; *cu* – cow; *sterteth* – starts; *verteth* – farts;
murie – merrily; *thu* – thou; *swik* – stop; *naver* – never; *nu* – now.)

William Morris (1834–1896)

Summer Dawn

The impact of the countryside on Morris is perhaps best seen in his enduringly popular textile designs, which feature flowers, fruit, leaves and birds arranged into stunningly decorative patterns.

Pray but one prayer for me 'twixt thy closed lips;
   Think but one thought of me up in the stars.
The summer night waneth, the morning light slips,
   Faint and grey 'twixt the leaves of the aspen,
     betwixt the cloud-bars,
That are patiently waiting there for the dawn:
   Patient and colourless, though Heaven's gold
Waits to float through them along with the sun.
Far out in the meadows, above the young corn,
   The heavy elms wait, and restless and cold
The uneasy wind rises; the roses are dun;
Through the long twilight they pray for the dawn,
Round the lone house in the midst of the corn.
   Speak but one word to me over the corn,
    Over the tender, bowed locks of the corn.

William Blake (1757–1827)

To Summer

O thou, who passest thro' our valleys in
Thy strength, curb thy fierce steeds, allay the heat
That flames from their large nostrils! thou, O Summer,
Oft pitched'st here thy golden tent, and oft
Beneath our oaks hast slept, while we beheld
With joy, thy ruddy limbs and flourishing hair.

Beneath our thickest shades we oft have heard
Thy voice, when noon upon his fervid car
Rode o'er the deep of heaven; beside our springs
Sit down, and in our mossy valleys, on
Some bank beside a river clear, throw thy
Silk draperies off, and rush into the stream:
Our valleys love the Summer in his pride.

Our bards are fam'd who strike the silver wire:
Our youth are bolder than the southern swains:
Our maidens fairer in the sprightly dance:
We lack not songs, nor instruments of joy,
Nor echoes sweet, nor waters clear as heaven,
Nor laurel wreaths against the sultry heat.

Dylan Thomas (1914–1953)

Fern Hill

Now as I was young and easy under the apple boughs
About the lilting house and happy as the grass was green,
    The night above the dingle starry,
        Time let me hail and climb
      Golden in the heydays of his eyes,
And honoured among wagons I was prince of the apple towns
And once below a time I lordly had the trees and leaves
        Trail with daisies and barley
      Down the rivers of the windfall light.

And as I was green and carefree, famous among the barns
About the happy yard and singing as the farm was home,
    In the sun that is young once only,
        Time let me play and be
      Golden in the mercy of his means,
And green and golden I was huntsman and herdsman, the calves
Sang to my horn, the foxes on the hills barked clear and cold,
        And the sabbath rang slowly
      In the pebbles of the holy streams.

All the sun long it was running, it was lovely, the hay
Fields high as the house, the tunes from the chimneys, it was air
    And playing, lovely and watery
        And fire green as grass.
      And nightly under the simple stars
As I rode to sleep the owls were bearing the farm away,
All the moon long I heard, blessed among stables, the nightjars
        Flying with the ricks, and the horses
          Flashing into the dark.

And then to awake, and the farm, like a wanderer white
With the dew, come back, the cock on his shoulder: it was all
    Shining, it was Adam and maiden,
        The sky gathered again
    And the sun grew round that very day.
So it must have been after the birth of the simple light
In the first, spinning place, the spellbound horses walking warm
    Out of the whinnying green stable
        On to the fields of praise.

And honoured among foxes and pheasants by the gay house
Under the new made clouds and happy as the heart was long,
    In the sun born over and over,
        I ran my heedless ways,
    My wishes raced through the house high hay
And nothing I cared, at my sky blue trades, that time allows
In all his tuneful turning so few and such morning songs
    Before the children green and golden
        Follow him out of grace,

Nothing I cared, in the lamb white days, that time would
  take me
Up to the swallow thronged loft by the shadow of my hand,
    In the moon that is always rising,
        Nor that riding to sleep
    I should hear him fly with the high fields
And wake to the farm forever fled from the childless land.
Oh as I was young and easy in the mercy of his means,
        Time held me green and dying
    Though I sang in my chains like the sea.

William Shakespeare (1564–1616)

Sonnet 18

Although often quoted as a classic paean to the season, in this sonnet the British summer comes off rather badly when compared to the poet's lover, as the darling buds are buffeted by stiff winds.

Shall I compare thee to a summer's day?
Thou art more lovely and more temperate:
Rough winds do shake the darling buds of May,
And summer's lease hath all too short a date;
Sometimes too hot the eye of heaven shines,
And often is his gold complexion dimmed;
And every fair from fair sometime declines,
By chance or nature's changing course untrimmed;
But thy eternal summer shall not fade,
Nor lose possession of that fair thou ow'st;
Nor shall death brag thou wand'rest in his shade,
When in eternal lines to Time thou grow'st:
    So long as men can breathe, or eyes can see,
    So long lives this, and this gives life to thee.

Dante Gabriel Rossetti (1828–1882)

A Half-Way Pause

The turn of noontide has begun.
   In the weak breeze the sunshine yields.
   There is a bell upon the fields.
On the long hedgerow's tangled run
   A low white cottage intervenes:
   Against the wall a blind man leans,
And sways his face to have the sun.

Our horses' hoofs stir in the road,
   Quiet and sharp. Light hath a song
   Whose silence, being heard, seems long.
The point of noon maketh abode,
   And will not be at once gone through.
   The sky's deep colour saddens you,
And the heat weighs a dreamy load.

Matthew Arnold (1822–1888)

The Scholar-Gypsy [extract]

Go, for they call you, shepherd, from the hill;
    Go, shepherd, and untie the wattled cotes!
        No longer leave thy wistful flock unfed,
    Nor let thy bawling fellows rack their throats,
        Nor the cropped herbage shoot another head.
            But when the fields are still,
    And the tired men and dogs all gone to rest,
        And only the white sheep are sometimes seen
        Cross and recross the strips of moon-blanched green.
    Come, shepherd, and again begin the quest!

Here, where the reaper was at work of late—
    In this high field's dark corner, where he leaves
        His coat, his basket, and his earthen cruse,
    And in the sun all morning binds the sheaves,
        Then here, at noon, comes back his stores to use—
            Here will I sit and wait,
    While to my ear from uplands far away
        The bleating of the folded flocks is borne,
        With distant cries of reapers in the corn—
    All the live murmur of a summer's day.

Screened is this nook o'er the high, half-reaped field,
    And here till sun-down, shepherd! will I be.
        Through the thick corn the scarlet poppies peep,
    And round green roots and yellowing stalks I see
        Pale pink convolvulus in tendrils creep;
            And air-swept lindens yield
        Their scent, and rustle down their perfumed showers

Of bloom on the bent grass where I am laid,
And bower me from the August sun with shade;
And the eye travels down to Oxford's towers.

Ebenezer Jones (1820–1860)

High Summer

The critics savaged Jones's work during his lifetime and the Daily
Telegraph's *Christopher Howse called him 'the worst poet in the world'
as recently as 2010.[1] In spite of this abuse, his thoughts on a hot day in
the countryside are pleasantly evocative.*

I never wholly feel that summer is high,
However green the trees, or loud the birds,
However movelessly eye-winking herds
Stand in field ponds, or under large trees lie,
Till I do climb all cultured pastures by,
That hedged by hedgerows studiously fretted trim,
Smile like a lady's face with lace laced prim,
And on some moor or hill that seeks the sky
Lonely and nakedly, – utterly lie down,
And feel the sunshine throbbing on body and limb,
My drowsy brain in pleasant drunkenness swim,
Each rising thought sink back and dreamily drown,
Smiles creep o'er my face, and smother my lips, and cloy,
Each muscle sink to itself, and separately enjoy.

---

1   'Happy birthday, Ebenezer Jones, the worst poet in the world', by Christopher Howse
    (*Daily Telegraph* blogs, 19 January 2010)

Edward Thomas (1878–1917)

July

Naught moves but clouds, and in the glassy lake
Their doubles and the shadow of my boat.
The boat itself stirs only when I break
This drowse of heat and solitude afloat
To prove if what I see be bird or mote,
Or learn if yet the shore woods be awake.

Long hours since dawn grew, – spread, – and passed on high
And deep below, – I have watched the cool reeds hung
Over images more cool in imaged sky:
Nothing there was worth thinking of so long;
All that the ring-doves say, far leaves among,
Brims my mind with content thus still to lie.

William Wordsworth (1770–1850)

Lines Composed a Few Miles Above Tintern Abbey [extract]

This poem sees Wordsworth far from the Lake District, with which he is so strongly associated, and gazing instead upon the still beautiful ruins of the Cistercian abbey of Tintern in Monmouthshire, South Wales.

Five years have past; five summers, with the length
Of five long winters! and again I hear
These waters, rolling from their mountain-springs
With a soft inland murmur. Once again

Do I behold these steep and lofty cliffs,
That on a wild secluded scene impress
Thoughts of more deep seclusion; and connect
The landscape with the quiet of the sky.
The day is come when I again repose
Here, under this dark sycamore, and view
These plots of cottage – ground, these orchard-tufts,
Which at this season, with their unripe fruits,
Are clad in one green hue, and lose themselves
'Mid groves and copses. Once again I see
These hedgerows, hardly hedgerows, little lines
Of sportive wood run wild; these pastoral farms,
Green to the very door; and wreaths of smoke
Sent up, in silence, from among the trees!
With some uncertain notice, as might seem
Of vagrant dwellers in the houseless woods,
Or of some Hermit's cave, where by his fire
The Hermit sits alone.

William Shakespeare (1564–1616)

Ariel's song from *The Tempest*

Where the bee sucks, there suck I:
In a cowslip's bell I lie;
There I couch when owls do cry.
On the bat's back I do fly
After summer merrily.
Merrily, merrily shall I live now
Under the blossom that hangs on the bough.

William Blake (1757–1827)

Laughing Song

When the green woods laugh with the voice of joy,
And the dimpling stream runs laughing by;
When the air does laugh with our merry wit,
And the green hill laughs with the noise of it.

When the meadows laugh with lively green,
And the grasshopper laughs in the merry scene,
When Mary and Susan and Emily,
With their sweet round mouths sing 'Ha, ha he!'

When the painted birds laugh in the shade,
Where our table with cherries and nuts is spread:
Come live, and be merry, and join with me,
To sing the sweet chorus of 'Ha, ha, he!'

Henry Howard, Earl of Surrey (c.1517–1547)

The Soote Season

Howard lived at the turbulent heart of Tudor politics. He boasted Edward I and Edward III as ancestors and Anne Boleyn as a cousin, and the poet Thomas Wyatt was among his closest friends. It was a dangerous time for great men, though, and he lost his head when an ageing and paranoid Henry VIII suspected him of designs on the crown.

The soote season, that bud and blome furth bringes,
With grene hath clad the hill and eke the vale;

The nightingale with fethers new she sings;
The turtle to her make hath tolde her tale.
Somer is come, for every spray nowe springs;
The hart hath hong his olde hed on the pale;
The buck in brake his winter cote he flinges;
The fishes flote with newe repaired scale;
The adder all her sloughe away she slinges;
The swift swallow pursueth the flyes smale;
The busy bee her honye now she minges;
Winter is worne that was the flowers bale.
And thus I see among these pleasant things
Eche care decayes, and my sorrow springs.

John Milton (1608–1674)

L'Allegro

But come thou goddess fair and free,
In heav'n yclep'd Euphrosyne,
And by men, heart-easing Mirth,
Whom lovely Venus at a birth
With two sister Graces more
To Ivy-crowned Bacchus bore;
Or whether (as some sager sing)
The frolic wind that breathes the spring,
Zephyr, with Aurora playing,
As he met her once a-Maying,
There on beds of violets blue,
And fresh-blown roses wash'd in dew,
Fill'd her with thee, a daughter fair,
So buxom, blithe, and debonair.

Haste thee, nymph, and bring with thee
Jest and youthful Jollity,
Quips and cranks, and wanton wiles,
Nods, and becks, and wreathed smiles,
Such as hang on Hebe's cheek,
And love to live in dimple sleek;
Sport that wrinkled Care derides,
And Laughter holding both his sides.
Come, and trip it as ye go
On the light fantastic toe,
And in thy right hand lead with thee,
The mountain-nymph, sweet Liberty;
And if I give thee honour due,
Mirth, admit me of thy crew
To live with her, and live with thee,
In unreproved pleasures free;
To hear the lark begin his flight,
And singing startle the dull night,
From his watch-tower in the skies,
Till the dappled dawn doth rise;
Then to come in spite of sorrow,
And at my window bid good-morrow,
Through the sweet-briar, or the vine,
Or the twisted eglantine;
While the cock with lively din,
Scatters the rear of darkness thin,
And to the stack, or the barn door,
Stoutly struts his dames before;
Oft list'ning how the hounds and horn
Cheerly rouse the slumb'ring morn,
From the side of some hoar hill,
Through the high wood echoing shrill.
Sometime walking, not unseen,

By hedgerow elms, on hillocks green,
Right against the eastern gate,
Where the great Sun begins his state,
Rob'd in flames, and amber light,
The clouds in thousand liveries dight.
While the ploughman near at hand,
Whistles o'er the furrow'd land,
And the milkmaid singeth blithe,
And the mower whets his scythe,
And every shepherd tells his tale
Under the hawthorn in the dale.
Straight mine eye hath caught new pleasures
Whilst the landscape round it measures,
Russet lawns, and fallows gray,
Where the nibbling flocks do stray;
Mountains on whose barren breast
The labouring clouds do often rest;
Meadows trim with daisies pied,
Shallow brooks, and rivers wide.
Towers, and battlements it sees
Bosom'd high in tufted trees,
Where perhaps some beauty lies,
The cynosure of neighbouring eyes.

John Keats (1795–1821)

Ode to a Nightingale

My heart aches, and a drowsy numbness pains
   My sense, as though of hemlock I had drunk,
Or emptied some dull opiate to the drains
   One minute past, and Lethe-wards had sunk:
'Tis not through envy of thy happy lot,
   But being too happy in thine happiness,—
      That thou, light-winged Dryad of the trees
        In some melodious plot
   Of beechen green, and shadows numberless,
     Singest of summer in full-throated ease.

O, for a draught of vintage! that hath been
   Cooled a long age in the deep-delvèd earth,
Tasting of Flora and the country green,
   Dance, and Provençal song, and sunburnt mirth!
O for a beaker full of the warm South,
   Full of the true, the blushful Hippocrene,
      With beaded bubbles winking at the brim,
        And purple-stainèd mouth;
   That I might drink, and leave the world unseen,
     And with thee fade away into the forest dim:

Fade far away, dissolve, and quite forget
   What thou among the leaves hast never known,
The weariness, the fever, and the fret
   Here, where men sit and hear each other groan;
Where palsy shakes a few, sad, last grey hairs,
   Where youth grows pale, and spectre-thin, and dies;
     Where but to think is to be full of sorrow

And leaden-eyed despairs,
Where Beauty cannot keep her lustrous eyes,
Or new Love pine at them beyond tomorrow.

Away! away! for I will fly to thee,
Not charioted by Bacchus and his pards,
But on the viewless wings of Poesy,
Though the dull brain perplexes and retards:
Already with thee! tender is the night,
And haply the Queen-Moon is on her throne,
Clustered around by all her starry Fays;
But here there is no light,
Save what from heaven is with the breezes blown
Through verdurous glooms and winding mossy ways.

I cannot see what flowers are at my feet,
Nor what soft incense hangs upon the boughs,
But, in embalmèd darkness, guess each sweet
Wherewith the seasonable month endows
The grass, the thicket, and the fruit tree wild;
White hawthorn, and the pastoral eglantine;
Fast fading violets covered up in leaves;
And mid-May's eldest child,
The coming musk-rose, full of dewy wine,
The murmurous haunt of flies on summer eves.

Darkling I listen; and for many a time
I have been half in love with easeful Death,
Called him soft names in many a musèd rhyme,
To take into the air my quiet breath;
Now more than ever seems it rich to die,
To cease upon the midnight with no pain,
While thou art pouring forth thy soul abroad

In such an ecstasy!
Still wouldst thou sing, and I have ears in vain—
   To thy high requiem become a sod.

Thou wast not born for death, immortal Bird!
   No hungry generations tread thee down;
The voice I hear this passing night was heard
   In ancient days by emperor and clown:
Perhaps the selfsame song that found a path
   Through the sad heart of Ruth, when, sick for home,
      She stood in tears amid the alien corn;
         The same that ofttimes hath
   Charmed magic casements, opening on the foam
   Of perilous seas, in faery lands forlorn.

Forlorn! the very word is like a bell
   To toll me back from thee to my sole self!
Adieu! the fancy cannot cheat so well
   As she is famed to do, deceiving elf.
Adieu! adieu! thy plaintive anthem fades
   Past the near meadows, over the still stream,
      Up the hillside; and now 'tis buried deep
         In the next valley-glades:
   Was it a vision, or a waking dream?
      Fled is that music: – Do I wake or sleep?

The Seaside

Shakespeare called this island nation a 'precious stone set in the silver sea', and the coast has inspired bards throughout history. Its infinite variety encompasses gentle, tide-lapped bays, shingle beaches and dramatic cliffs. The seaside has long held a venerated and unassailable position as the location of leisure in the British imagination, whether or not the reality of sandy sandwiches and chattering teeth lives up to the dream.

John Masefield (1878–1967)

Sea-Fever

Masefield was well qualified to write about the coast, having spent several years at sea in his youth.

I must down to the seas again, to the lonely sea and the sky,
And all I ask is a tall ship and a star to steer her by,
And the wheel's kick and the wind's song
   and the white sail's shaking,
And a grey mist on the sea's face and a grey dawn breaking.

I must down to the seas again, for the call of the running tide
Is a wild call and a clear call that may not be denied;
And all I ask is a windy day with the white clouds flying,
And the flung spray and the blown spume,
   and the sea-gulls crying.

I must down to the seas again, to the vagrant gypsy life,
To the gull's way and the whale's way where the wind's like a
   whetted knife;
And all I ask is a merry yarn from a laughing fellow-rover,
And quiet sleep and a sweet dream when the long trick's over.

Dylan Thomas (1914–1953)

We lying by seasand

We lying by seasand, watching yellow
And the grave sea, mock who deride
Who follow the red rivers, hollow
Alcove of words out of cicada shade,
For in this yellow grave of sand and sea
A calling for colour calls with the wind
That's grave and gay as grave and sea
Sleeping on either hand.
The lunar silences, the silent tide
Lapping the still canals, the dry tide-master
Ribbed between desert and water storm,
Should cure our ills of the water
With a one-coloured calm;
The heavenly music over the sand
Sounds with the grains as they hurry
Hiding the golden mountains and mansions
Of the grave, gay seaside land.
Bound by a sovereign strip, we lie,
Watch yellow, wish for wind to blow away
The strata of the shore and leave red rock;
But wishes breed not, neither
Can we fend off the rock arrival,
Lie watching yellow until the golden weather
Breaks, O my heart's blood, like a heart and hill.

John Betjeman (1906–1984)

A Bay in Anglesey

*Betjeman's work on the Shell motoring guides to the counties of England
enabled him to acquaint himself intimately with the British countryside,
which forms the backdrop to some of his best-loved poetry.*

The sleepy sound of a tea-time tide
Slaps at the rocks the sun has dried,

Too lazy, almost, to sink and lift
Round low peninsulas pink with thrift.

The water, enlarging shells and sand,
Grows greener emerald out from land

And brown over shadowy shelves below
The waving forests of seaweed show.

Here at my feet in the short cliff grass
Are shells, dried bladderwrack, broken glass,

Pale blue squills and yellow rock roses.
The next low ridge that we climb discloses

One more field for the sheep to graze
While, scarcely seen on this hottest of days,

Far to the eastward, over there,
Snowdon rises in pearl-grey air.

Multiple lark-song, whispering bents,
The thymy, turfy and salty scents

And filling in, brimming in, sparkling and free
The sweet susurration of incoming sea.

Coventry Patmore (1823–1896)

Magna est Veritas

Here, in this little Bay,
Full of tumultuous life and great repose,
Where, twice a day,
The purposeless, glad ocean comes and goes,
Under high cliffs, and far from the huge town,
I sit me down.
For want of me the world's course will not fail;
When all its work is done, the lie shall rot;
The truth is great, and shall prevail,
When none cares whether it prevail or not.

W. H. Auden (1907–1973)

On This Island

Look, stranger, on this island now
The leaping light for your delight discovers,
Stand stable here
And silent be
That through the channels of the ear
May wander like a river
The swaying sound of the sea.

Here at the small field's ending pause
Where the chalk wall falls to the foam, and its tall ledges
Oppose the pluck
And knock of the tide,
And the shingle scrambles after the suck-
ing surf,
And the gull lodges
A moment on its sheer side.

Far off like floating seeds the ships
Diverge on urgent voluntary errands,
And the full view
Indeed may enter
And move in memory as now these clouds do,
That pass the harbour mirror
And all the summer through the water saunter.

Edwin Muir (1887–1959)

Childhood

Muir was born and spent much of his childhood on the remote Scottish island of Orkney, which came to symbolize an unspoiled Eden in his poetry.

Long time he lay upon the sunny hill,
  To his father's house below securely bound.
Far off the silent, changing sound was still,
  With the black islands lying thick around.

He saw each separate height, each vaguer hue,
  Where the massed islands rolled in mist away,
And though all ran together in his view
  He knew that unseen straits between them lay.

Often he wondered what new shores were there.
  In thought he saw the still light on the sand,
The shallow water clear in tranquil air,
  And walked through it in joy from strand to strand.

Over the sound a ship so slow would pass
  That in the black hill's gloom it seemed to lie.
The evening sound was smooth like sunken glass,
  And time seemed finished ere the ship passed by.

Grey tiny rocks slept round him where he lay,
  Moveless as they, more still as evening came,
The grasses threw straight shadows far away,
  And from the house his mother called his name.

Frances Cornford (1886–1960)

The Coast: Norfolk

Cornford's husband was named Francis, so her family differentiated between them by calling them by their initials, so she was known as 'FCC' and he as 'FMC'.

As on the highway's quiet edge
He mows the grass beside the hedge,
The old man has for company
The distant, grey, salt-smelling sea,
A poppied field, a cow and calf,
The finches on the telegraph.

Across his faded back a hone,
He slowly, slowly scythes alone
In silence of the wind-soft air,
With ladies' bedstraw everywhere,
With whitened corn, and tarry poles,
And far-off gulls like risen souls.

Afternoon

No collection of poems about the English afternoon would be complete without mention of the sacred meal of tea, immortalized by Rupert Brooke in 'The Old Vicarage, Grantchester'.

Rupert Brooke (1887–1915)

The Old Vicarage, Grantchester [extract]

Ah God! to see the branches stir
Across the moon at Grantchester!
To smell the thrilling-sweet and rotten
Unforgettable, unforgotten
River-smell, and hear the breeze
Sobbing in the little trees.
Say, do the elm-clumps greatly stand
Still guardians of that holy land?
The chestnuts shade, in reverend dream,
The yet unacademic stream?
Is dawn a secret shy and cold
Anadyomene, silver-gold?
And sunset still a golden sea
From Haslingfield to Madingley?
And after, ere the night is born,
Do hares come out about the corn?
Oh, is the water sweet and cool,
Gentle and brown, above the pool?
And laughs the immortal river still
Under the mill, under the mill?
Say, is there Beauty yet to find?
And Certainty? and Quiet kind?
Deep meadows yet, for to forget
The lies, and truths, and pain? . . . Oh! yet
Stands the Church clock at ten to three?
And is there honey still for tea?

Edward Thomas (1878–1917)

Adlestrop

Thomas's poems were collected following his death on the Western Front in 1917, and found a wide and appreciative audience only after the Second World War when their evocation of rural southern England already had a nostalgic allure.

Yes, I remember Adlestrop –
The name, because one afternoon
Of heat the express-train drew up there
Unwontedly. It was late June.

The steam hissed. Someone cleared his throat.
No one left and no one came
On the bare platform. What I saw
Was Adlestrop—only the name

And willows, willow-herb, and grass,
And meadowsweet, and haycocks dry,
No whit less still and lonely fair
Than the high cloudlets in the sky.

And for that minute a blackbird sang
Close by, and round him, mistier,
Farther and farther, all the birds
Of Oxfordshire and Gloucestershire.

W. H. Davies (1871–1940)

Leisure

Davies was a heavy drinker living rough in London when he wrote many of his most famous poems, so their fresh, rural flavour is something of a surprise.

What is this life if, full of care,
We have no time to stand and stare?—

No time to stand beneath the boughs,
And stare as long as sheep or cows:

No time to see, when woods we pass,
Where squirrels hide their nuts in grass:

No time to see, in broad daylight,
Streams full of stars, like skies at night:

No time to turn at Beauty's glance,
And watch her feet, how they can dance:

No time to wait till her mouth can
Enrich that smile her eyes began?

A poor life this if, full of care,
We have no time to stand and stare.

Lewis Carroll (1832–1898)

All in the Golden Afternoon

Here, Carroll claims that his much-loved story Alice in Wonderland
was the product of a lazy afternoon spent boating.

All in the golden afternoon
    Full leisurely we glide;
For both our oars, with little skill,
    By little arms are plied,
While little hands make vain pretence
    Our wanderings to guide.

Ah, cruel Three! In such an hour,
    Beneath such dreamy weather,
To beg a tale of breath too weak
    To stir the tiniest feather!
Yet what can one poor voice avail
    Against three tongues together?

Imperious Prima flashes forth
    Her edict 'to begin it':
In gentler tones Secunda hopes
    'There will be nonsense in it!'
While Tertia interrupts the tale
    Not more than once a minute.

Anon, to sudden silence won,
    In fancy they pursue
The dream-child moving through a land
    Of wonders wild and new,
In friendly chat with bird or beast –
    And half believe it true.

And ever, as the story drained
    The wells of fancy dry,
And faintly strove that weary one
    To put the subject by,
'The rest next time–' 'It is next time!'
    The happy voices cry.

Thus grew the tale of Wonderland:
    Thus slowly, one by one,
Its quaint events were hammered out –
    And now the tale is done,
And home we steer, a merry crew,
    Beneath the setting sun.

Alice! A childish story take,
    And, with a gentle hand,
Lay it where Childhood's dreams are twined
    In Memory's mystic band,
Like pilgrim's wither'd wreath of flowers
    Pluck'd in a far-off land.

Rivers

'Messing about on the river' is a quintessentially British pastime, and poets are evidently not immune to its charms. The sights and sounds of British waterways, from babbling brooks to the stately Thames, are here celebrated.

Alfred, Lord Tennyson (1809–1892)

Song of the Brook

These verses are thought to have been inspired by the brook that flows through the village of Somersby in the Lincolnshire Wolds, where Tennyson spent his boyhood.

I come from haunts of coot and hern,
    I make a sudden sally,
And sparkle out among the fern,
    To bicker down a valley.

By thirty hills I hurry down,
    Or slip between the ridges,
By twenty thorps, a little town,
    And half a hundred bridges.

Till last by Philip's farm I flow
    To join the brimming river,
For men may come and men may go,
    But I go on for ever.

I chatter over stony ways,
    In little sharps and trebles,
I bubble into eddying bays,
    I babble on the pebbles.

With many a curve my banks I fret
    By many a field and fallow,
And many a fairy foreland set
    With willow-weed and mallow.

I chatter, chatter, as I flow
   To join the brimming river,
For men may come and men may go,
   But I go on for ever.

I wind about, and in and out,
   With here a blossom sailing,
And here and there a lusty trout,
   And here and there a grayling,

And here and there a foamy flake
   Upon me, as I travel
With many a silvery waterbreak
   Above the golden gravel,

And draw them all along, and flow
   To join the brimming river,
For men may come and men may go,
   But I go on for ever.

I steal by lawns and grassy plots,
   I slide by hazel covers;
I move the sweet forget-me-nots
   That grow for happy lovers.

I slip, I slide, I gloom, I glance,
   Among my skimming swallows;
I make the netted sunbeam dance
   Against my sandy shallows.

I murmur under moon and stars
   In brambly wildernesses;

I linger by my shingly bars;
   I loiter round my cresses;

And out again I curve and flow
   To join the brimming river,
For men may come and men may go,
   But I go on for ever.

George Crabbe (1754–1832)

The Borough [extract]

*Crabbe's depictions of rural life won him praise from Lord Byron, who
called him, 'nature's sternest painter, yet the best'.*

With ceaseless motion comes and goes the tide,
Flowing, it fills the channel vast and wide;
Then back to sea, with strong majestic sweep
It rolls, in ebb yet terrible and deep;
Here samphire-banks and salt-wort bound the flood,
There stakes and sea-weeds withering on the mud;
And higher up, a ridge of all things base,
Which some strong tide has rolled upon the place.
   Thy gentle river boasts its pygmy boat,
Urged on by pains, half grounded, half afloat;
While at her stern an angler takes his stand,
And marks the fish he purposes to land
From that clear space, where, in the cheerful ray
Of the warm sun, the sealy people play.

William Wordsworth (1770–1850)

The Prelude [extract]

Was it for this
That one, the fairest of all rivers, loved
To blend his murmurs with my nurse's song,
And from his alder shades and rocky falls,
And from his fords and shallows, sent a voice
That flowed along my dreams? For this didst thou,
O Derwent, travelling over the green plains
Near my 'sweet Birthplace', didst thou, beauteous stream
Make ceaseless music through the night and day,
Which with its steady cadence, tempering
Our human waywardness, composed my thoughts
To more than infant softness, giving me
Among the fretful dwelling of mankind,
A knowledge, a dim earnest, of the calm
Which Nature breathes among the hills and groves?
Beloved Derwent, fairest of all streams,
Was it for this that I, a four years' child,
A naked boy, among thy silent pools
Made one long bathing of a summer's day,
Basked in the sun, or plunged into thy streams,
Alternate, all a summer's day, or coursed
Over the sandy fields, and dashed the flowers
Of yellow grunsel; or, when crag and hill,
The woods, and distant Skiddaw's lofty height,
Were bronzed with a deep radiance, stood alone
A naked savage in the thunder shower?

Sir John Denham (1615–1669)

Cooper's Hill [extract]

Denham lived in Egham in Surrey, and in this poem he celebrates the
Thames Valley landscape around his home. It is thought to be the earliest
poem in English celebrating a specific location.

My eye descending from the Hill, surveys
Where Thames amongst the wanton vallies strays.
Thames, the most lov'd of all the Oceans sons,
By his old Sire to his embraces runs,
Hasting to pay his tribute to the Sea,
Like mortal life to meet Eternity.
Though with those streams he no resemblance hold,
Whose foam is Amber, and their Gravel Gold;
His genuine, and less guilty wealth t'explore,
Search not his bottom, but survey his shore;
Ore which he kindly spreads his spacious wing,
And hatches plenty for th'ensuing Spring.
Nor then destroys it with too fond a stay,
Like Mothers which their Infants overlay.
Nor with a sudden and impetuous wave,
Like profuse Kings, resumes the wealth he gave.
No unexpected inundations spoyl
The mowers hopes, nor mock the plowmans toyl:
But God-like his unwearied Bounty flows;
First loves to do, then loves the Good he does.
Nor are his Blessings to his banks confin'd,
But free, and common, as the Sea or Wind;
When he to boast, or to disperse his stores
Full of the tributes of his grateful shores,
Visits the world, and in his flying towers

Brings home to us, and makes both Indies ours;
Finds wealth where 'tis, bestows it where it wants,
Cities in deserts, woods in Cities plants.
So that to us no thing, no place is strange,
While his fair bosom is the worlds exchange.
O could I flow like thee, and make thy stream
My great example, as it is my theme!
Though deep, yet clear, though gentle, yet not dull,
Strong without rage, without ore-flowing full.

AUTUMN

The vibrant colours of the countryside as the leaves turn makes autumn in Britain a magical and inspiring time, and some of the most famous pastoral verse in English celebrates this season of change. Autumn blows in with the harvest and, although winter must be hard on his heels, it is often a time of late warmth and pleasant weather.

William Blake (1757–1827)

To Autumn

Blake's 'season' poems appeared in Poetical Sketches *(1783) and are among his earliest works.*

O Autumn, laden with fruit, and stainèd
With the blood of the grape, pass not, but sit
Beneath my shady roof; there thou may'st rest,
And tune thy jolly voice to my fresh pipe,
And all the daughters of the year shall dance!
Sing now the lusty song of fruits and flowers.

'The narrow bud opens her beauties to
The sun, and love runs in her thrilling veins;
Blossoms hang round the brows of morning, and
Flourish down the bright cheek of modest eve,
Till clust'ring Summer breaks forth into singing,
And feather'd clouds strew flowers round her head.

'The spirits of the air live on the smells
Of fruit; and joy, with pinions light, roves round
The gardens, or sits singing in the trees.'
Thus sang the jolly Autumn as he sat;
Then rose, girded himself, and o'er the bleak
Hills fled from our sight; but left his golden load.

John Keats (1795–1821)

To Autumn

Keats is another London-born poet famed for his verses about the glories of the countryside, although contemporary critics pilloried him as part of a 'Cockney School' of poetry.

Season of mists and mellow fruitfulness,
    Close bosom-friend of the maturing sun,
Conspiring with him how to load and bless
    With fruit the vines that round the thatch-eaves run;
To bend with apples the mossed cottage-trees,
    And fill all fruit with ripeness to the core;
        To swell the gourd, and plump the hazel shells
    With a sweet kernel; to set budding more,
And still more, later flowers for the bees,
Until they think warm days will never cease,
        For Summer has o'er-brimm'd their clammy cells.

Who hath not seen thee oft amid thy store?
    Sometimes whoever seeks abroad may find
Thee sitting careless on a granary floor,
    Thy hair soft-lifted by the winnowing wind;
Or on a half-reaped furrow sound asleep,
    Drowsed with the fume of poppies, while thy hook
        Spares the next swath and all its twinèd flowers;
    And sometimes like a gleaner thou dost keep
Steady thy laden head across a brook;
Or by a cider-press, with patient look,
        Thou watchest the last oozings hours by hours.

Where are the songs of Spring? Ay, where are they?
 Think not of them, thou hast thy music too, –
While barrèd clouds bloom the soft-dying day,
 And touch the stubble-plains with rosy hue:
Then in a wailful choir the small gnats mourn
 Among the river sallows, borne aloft
  Or sinking as the light wind lives or dies;
And full-grown lambs loud bleat from hilly bourn;
Hedge-crickets sing; and now with treble soft
The red-breast whistles from a garden-croft;
  And gathering swallows twitter in the skies.

Edward Thomas (1878–1917)

The Lane

Some day, I think, there will be people enough
In Froxfield to pick all the blackberries
Out of the hedges of Green Lane, the straight
Broad lane where now September hides herself
In bracken and blackberry, harebell and dwarf gorse.
Today, where yesterday a hundred sheep
Were nibbling, halcyon bells shake to the sway
Of waters that no vessel ever sailed ...
It is a kind of spring: the chaffinch tries
His song. For heat it is like summer too.
This might be winter's quiet. While the glint
Of hollies dark in the swollen hedges lasts—
One mile—and those bells ring, little I know
Or heed if time be still the same, until
The lane ends and once more all is the same.

William Shakespeare (1564–1616)

Sonnet 73

*Although Shakespeare spent most of his working life in London, there is
no doubt that his upbringing in Stratford-upon-Avon equipped him with
a love for and understanding of the English countryside that enabled
him to write unparalleled pastoral poems.*

That time of year thou may'st in me behold
When yellow leaves, or none, or few, do hang
Upon those boughs which shake against the cold,
Bare ruin'd choirs, where late the sweet birds sang.
In me thou see'st the twilight of such day,
As after sunset fadeth in the west,
Which by-and-by black night doth take away,
Death's second self, that seals up all in rest.
In me thou see'st the glowing of such fire
That on the ashes of his youth doth lie,
As the death-bed whereon it must expire
Consum'd with that which it was nourish'd by.
   This thou perceivest, which makes thy love more strong,
   To love that well which thou must leave ere long.

John Masefield (1878–1967)

Autumn Ploughing

After the ranks of stubble have lain bare,
And field mice and the finches' beaks have found
The last spilled seed corn left upon the ground;
And no more swallows miracle in air;

When the green tuft no longer hides the hare,
And dropping starling flights at evening come;
When birds, except the robin, have gone dumb,
And leaves are rustling downwards everywhere;

Then out, with the great horses, come the ploughs,
And all day long the slow procession goes,
Darkening the stubble fields with broadening strips.

Gray sea-gulls settle after to carouse:
Harvest prepares upon the harvest's close,
Before the blackbird pecks the scarlet hips.

Dylan Thomas (1914–1953)

Poem in October

It was my thirtieth year to heaven
Woke to my hearing from harbour and neighbour wood
  And the mussel pooled and the heron
     Priested shore
   The morning beckon
With water praying and call of seagull and rook
And the knock of sailing boats on the net webbed wall
   Myself to set foot
     That second
In the still sleeping town and set forth.

My birthday began with the water-
Birds and the birds of the winged trees flying my name
  Above the farms and the white horses
     And I rose
   In a rainy autumn
And walked abroad in a shower of all my days
High tide and the heron dived when I took the road
   Over the border
    And the gates
Of the town closed as the town awoke.

A springful of larks in a rolling
Cloud and the roadside bushes brimming with whistling
  Blackbirds and the sun of October
     Summery
    On the hill's shoulder,
Here were fond climates and sweet singers suddenly
Come in the morning where I wandered and listened

To the rain wringing
Wind blow cold
In the wood faraway under me.

Pale rain over the dwindling harbour
And over the sea wet church the size of a snail
With its horns through mist and the castle
Brown as owls
But all the gardens
Of spring and summer were blooming in the tall tales
Beyond the border and under the lark full cloud.
There could I marvel
My birthday
Away but the weather turned around.

It turned away from the blithe country
And down the other air and the blue altered sky
Streamed again a wonder of summer
With apples
Pears and red currants
And I saw in the turning so clearly a child's
Forgotten mornings when he walked with his mother
Through the parables
Of sunlight
And the legends of the green chapels

And the twice told fields of infancy
That his tears burned my cheeks and his heart moved in mine.
These were the woods the river and the sea
Where a boy
In the listening
Summertime of the dead whispered the truth of his joy
To the trees and the stones and the fish in the tide.

And the mystery
    Sang alive
Still in the water and singing birds.

And there could I marvel my birthday
Away but the weather turned around. And the true
   Joy of the long dead child sang burning
       In the sun.
   It was my thirtieth
Year to heaven stood there then in the summer noon
Though the town below lay leaved with October blood.
     O may my heart's truth
      Still be sung
   On this high hill in a year's turning.

A. E. Housman (1859–1936)

Tell me not here, it needs not saying

Tell me not here, it needs not saying,
  What tune the enchantress plays
In aftermaths of soft September
  Or under blanching mays,
For she and I were long acquainted
  And I knew all her ways.

On russet floors, by waters idle,
  The pine lets fall its cone;
The cuckoo shouts all day at nothing

In leafy dells alone;
And traveller's joy beguiles in autumn
   Hearts that have lost their own.

On acres of the seeded grasses
   The changing burnish heaves;
Or marshalled under moons of harvest
   Stand still all night the sheaves;
Or beeches strip in storms for winter
   And stain the wind with leaves.

Possess, as I possessed a season,
   The countries I resign,
Where over elmy plains the highway
   Would mount the hills and shine,
And full of shade the pillared forest
   Would murmur and be mine.

For nature, heartless, witless nature,
   Will neither care nor know
What stranger's feet may find the meadow
   And trespass there and go,
Nor ask amid the dews of morning
   If they are mine or no.

Edward Thomas (1878–1917)

October

The green elm with the one great bough of gold
Lets leaves into the grass slip, one by one, –
The short hill grass, the mushrooms small, milk-white,
Harebell and scabious and tormentil,
That blackberry and gorse, in dew and sun,
Bow down to; and the wind travels too light
To shake the fallen birch leaves from the fern;
The gossamers wander at their own will.
At heavier steps than birds' the squirrels scold.
The rich scene has grown fresh again and new
As Spring and to the touch is not more cool
Than it is warm to the gaze; and now I might
As happy be as earth is beautiful,
Were I some other or with earth could turn
In alternation of violet and rose,
Harebell and snowdrop, at their season due,
And gorse that has no time not to be gay.
But if this be not happiness, – who knows?
Some day I shall think this a happy day,
And this mood by the name of melancholy
Shall no more blackened and obscurèd be.

Donald Davie (1922–1995)

The Mushroom Gatherers

Strange walkers! See their processional
Perambulations under low boughs,
The birches white, and the green turf under.
These should be ghosts by moonlight wandering.

Their attitudes strange: the human tree
Slowly revolves on its bole. All around
Downcast looks; and the direct dreamer
Treads out in trance his lane, unwavering.

Strange decorum: so prodigal of bows,
Yet lost in thought and self-absorbed, they meet
Impassively, without acknowledgment.
A courteous nation, but unsociable.

Field full of folk, in their immunity
From human ills, crestfallen and serene.
Who would have thought these shades our lively friends?
Surely these acres are Elysian Fields.

John Betjeman (1906–1984)

Autumn 1964 (For Karen)

Betjeman was a passionate campaigner for the preservation of beautiful British buildings – including the nation's then unloved Victorian architecture – and the rural landscape. In his celebrated Daily Telegraph *columns he eulogized threatened and under-appreciated sites countrywide.*

Red apples hang like globes of light
   Against this pale November haze,
And now, although the mist is white,
   In half-an-hour a day of days
Will climb into its golden height
   And Sunday bells will ring its praise.

The sparkling flint, the darkling yew,
   The red brick, less intensely red
Than hawthorn berries bright with dew
   Or leaves of creeper still unshed,
The watery sky washed clean and new,
   Are all rejoicing with the dead.

The yellowing elm shows yet some green,
   The mellowing bells exultant sound:
Never have light and colour been
   So prodigally thrown around;
And in the bells the promise tells
   Of greater light where Love is found.

Percy Bysshe Shelley (1792–1822)

Ode to the West Wind

Shelley's Ode was written while he was living in Italy, close to Florence, though it evokes a blustery British autumn beautifully. Always a political radical, he here calls upon the wind to blow in revolutionary ideas as well as the new season.

I

O wild West Wind, thou breath of Autumn's being,
Thou, from whose unseen presence the leaves dead
Are driven, like ghosts from an enchanter fleeing,

Yellow, and black, and pale, and hectic red,
Pestilence-stricken multitudes: O thou,
Who chariotest to their dark wintry bed

The winged seeds, where they lie cold and low,
Each like a corpse within its grave, until
Thine azure sister of the Spring shall blow

Her clarion o'er the dreaming earth, and fill
(Driving sweet buds like flocks to feed in air)
With living hues and odours plain and hill:

Wild Spirit, which art moving everywhere;
Destroyer and preserver; hear, oh hear!

II

Thou on whose stream, mid the steep sky's commotion,
Loose clouds like earth's decaying leaves are shed,
Shook from the tangled boughs of Heaven and Ocean,

Angels of rain and lightning: there are spread
On the blue surface of thine aëry surge,
Like the bright hair uplifted from the head

Of some fierce Maenad, even from the dim verge
Of the horizon to the zenith's height,
The locks of the approaching storm. Thou dirge

Of the dying year, to which this closing night
Will be the dome of a vast sepulchre,
Vaulted with all thy congregated might

Of vapours, from whose solid atmosphere
Black rain, and fire, and hail will burst: oh hear!

III
Thou who didst waken from his summer dreams
The blue Mediterranean, where he lay,
Lull'd by the coil of his crystalline streams,

Beside a pumice isle in Baiae's bay,
And saw in sleep old palaces and towers
Quivering within the wave's intenser day,

All overgrown with azure moss and flowers
So sweet, the sense faints picturing them! Thou
For whose path the Atlantic's level powers

Cleave themselves into chasms, while far below
The sea-blooms and the oozy woods which wear
The sapless foliage of the ocean, know

Thy voice, and suddenly grow gray with fear,
And tremble and despoil themselves: oh hear!

IV
If I were a dead leaf thou mightest bear;
If I were a swift cloud to fly with thee;
A wave to pant beneath thy power, and share

The impulse of thy strength, only less free
Than thou, O uncontrollable! If even
I were as in my boyhood, and could be

The comrade of thy wanderings over Heaven,
As then, when to outstrip thy skiey speed
Scarce seem'd a vision; I would ne'er have striven

As thus with thee in prayer in my sore need.
Oh, lift me as a wave, a leaf, a cloud!
I fall upon the thorns of life! I bleed!

A heavy weight of hours has chain'd and bow'd
One too like thee: tameless, and swift, and proud.

V
Make me thy lyre, even as the forest is:
What if my leaves are falling like its own!
The tumult of thy mighty harmonies

Will take from both a deep, autumnal tone,
Sweet though in sadness. Be thou, Spirit fierce,
My spirit! Be thou me, impetuous one!

Drive my dead thoughts over the universe

Like wither'd leaves to quicken a new birth!
And, by the incantation of this verse,

Scatter, as from an unextinguish'd hearth
Ashes and sparks, my words among mankind!
Be through my lips to unawaken'd earth

The trumpet of a prophecy! O, Wind,
If Winter comes, can Spring be far behind?

Weather

Any group of poems about the British climate is bound to include several depictions of rain, although it is admittedly weather ill-suited to the tranquil composition of poetry. However, Wordsworth reminds us of the potential for the always unexpected delight of the rainbow in this island's often sodden sky. It is a sight guaranteed to make the most sombre of hearts skip.

William Shakespeare (1564–1616)

Feste's song from *Twelfth Night*

Twelfth Night was, as the title suggests, written for performance just after Christmas. Although the action is set in Illyria, on the Adriatic Sea, there is no doubt of Shakespeare's familiarity with a wet British winter.

When that I was and a little tiny boy,
    With hey, ho, the wind and the rain:
A foolish thing was but a toy,
    For the rain it raineth every day.

But when I came to man's estate,
    With hey, ho, the wind and the rain:
'Gainst knaves and thieves men shut their gate,
    For the rain it raineth every day.

But when I came, alas! to wive,
    With hey, ho, the wind and the rain,
By swaggering could I never thrive,
    For the rain it raineth every day.

But when I came unto my beds,
    With hey, ho, the wind and the rain:
With tosspots still had drunken heads,
    For the rain it raineth every day.

A great while ago the world begun,
    Hey, ho, the wind and the rain:
But that's all one, our play is done,
    And we'll strive to please you every day.

Donald Davie (1922–1995)

Tunstall Forest

Stillness! Down the dripping ride,
   The firebreak avenue
Of Tunstall Forest, at the side
   Of which we sought for you,
You did not come. The soft rain dropped,
   And quiet indeed we found:
No cars but ours, and ours was stopped,
   Rainfall the only sound.

And quiet is a lovely essence;
   Silence is of the tomb,
Austere though happy; but the tense
   Stillness did not come,
The deer did not, although they fed
   Perhaps nearby that day,
The liquid eye and elegant head
   No more than a mile away.

Ivor Gurney (1890–1937)

The Soaking

Gurney grew up in Gloucestershire and often returns in his writing to images of the countryside remembered from childhood, although he is now better remembered for his poems of the First World War.

The rain has come, and the earth must be very glad
Of its moisture, and the made roads all dust clad;
It lets a friendly veil down on the lucent dark,
And not of any bright ground thing shows any spark.

Tomorrow's grey morning will show cow-parsley,
Hung all with shining drops, and the river will be
Duller because of the all soddenness of things,
Till the skylark breaks his reluctance, hangs shaking, and sings.

Ted Hughes (1930–1998)

Wind

This house has been far out at sea all night,
The woods crashing through darkness, the booming hills,
Winds stampeding the fields under the window
Floundering black astride and blinding wet

Till day rose; then under an orange sky
The hills had new places, and wind wielded
Blade-light, luminous and emerald,
Flexing like the lens of a mad eye.

At noon I scaled along the house-side as far as
The coal-house door. I dared once to look up –
Through the brunt wind that dented the balls of my eyes
The tent of the hills drummed and strained its guyrope,

The fields quivering, the skyline a grimace,
At any second to bang and vanish with a flap:
The wind flung a magpie away and a black-
Back gull bent like an iron bar slowly. The house

Rang like some fine green goblet in the note
That any second would shatter it. Now deep
In chairs, in front of the great fire, we grip
Our hearts and cannot entertain book, thought,

Or each other. We watch the fire blazing,
And feel the roots of the house move, but sit on,
Seeing the window tremble to come in,
Hearing the stones cry out under the horizons.

William Wordsworth (1770–1850)

My Heart Leaps Up When I Behold

The British countryside was Wordsworth's greatest inspiration and it is through his eyes that we still see areas of great beauty including, of course, his beloved Lake District.

My heart leaps up when I behold
　　A rainbow in the sky:
So was it when my life began;
So is it now I am a man;
So be it when I shall grow old,
　　Or let me die!
The Child is father of the Man;
And I could wish my days to be
Bound each to each by natural piety.

Day's End

Sunsets and twilight have long inspired artists of all kinds. Gathered here are poems that celebrate the peace and enchantment of the British landscape as shadows lengthen, birds begin their evening chorus and night falls. Local folk tales and fairy stories have traditionally portrayed the 'in-between' time of dusk as one with magical potential, when other worlds are accessible, and poets are not immune to this strange charmed hour.

Thomas Gray (1716–1771)

Elegy Written in a Country Churchyard

The Curfew tolls the knell of parting day,
The lowing herd wind slowly o'er the lea,
The ploughman homeward plods his weary way,
And leaves the world to darkness and to me.

Now fades the glimmering landscape on the sight,
And all the air a solemn stillness holds,
Save where the beetle wheels his droning flight,
And drowsy tinklings lull the distant folds;

Save that from yonder ivy-mantled tow'r
The moping owl does to the moon complain
Of such, as wand'ring near her secret bower,
Molest her ancient solitary reign.

Beneath those rugged elms, that yew-tree's shade,
Where heaves the turf in many a mould'ring heap,
Each in his narrow cell for ever laid,
The rude Forefathers of the hamlet sleep.

The breezy call of incense-breathing morn,
The swallow twitt'ring from the straw-built shed,
The cock's shrill clarion, or the echoing horn,
No more shall rouse them from their lowly bed.

For them no more the blazing hearth shall burn,
Or busy housewife ply her evening care:
No children run to lisp their sire's return,
Or climb his knees the envied kiss to share.

Oft did the harvest to their sickle yield,
Their furrow oft the stubborn glebe has broke;
How jocund did they drive their team afield!
How bow'd the woods beneath their sturdy stroke!

Let not Ambition mock their useful toil,
Their homely joys, and destiny obscure;
Nor Grandeur hear with a disdainful smile,
The short and simple annals of the poor.

The boast of heraldry, the pomp of pow'r,
And all that beauty, all that wealth e'er gave,
Awaits alike th' inevitable hour.
The paths of glory lead but to the grave.

John Lucas Tupper (1824–1879)

A Sketch from Nature

This poem was composed in Sydenham Wood in 1849 and appeared in the first issue of the short-lived Pre-Raphaelite journal The Germ. *Tupper, like many of the Pre-Raphaelites, worked in several mediums and was best known as a sculptor.*

The air blows pure, for twenty miles,
    Over this vast countrié:
Over hill and wood and vale, it goeth,
    Over steeple, and stack, and tree:
And there's not a bird on the wind but knoweth
    How sweet these meadows be.
The swallows are flying beside the wood,

And the corbies are hoarsely crying;
And the sun at the end of the earth hath stood,
And, thorough the hedge and over the road,
    On the grassy slope is lying:
And the sheep are taking their supper-food
    While yet the rays are dying.

Sleepy shadows are filling the furrows,
    And giant-long shadows the trees are making;
And velvet soft are the woodland tufts,
And misty-grey the low-down crofts;
But the aspens there have gold-green tops,
    And the gold-green tops are shaking:
The spires are white in the sun's last light; –
And yet a moment ere he drops

Gazes the sun on the golden slopes.
Two sheep, afar from fold,
    Are on the hill-side straying,
With backs all silver, breasts all gold:
    The merle is something saying,
Something very very sweet: –
    'The day – the day – the day is done:'
There answereth a single bleat –
The air is cold, the sky is dimming,
And clouds are long like fishes swimming.

Rudyard Kipling (1865–1936)

The Way Through the Woods

They shut the road through the woods
Seventy years ago.
Weather and rain have undone it again,
And now you would never know
There was once a road through the woods
Before they planted the trees.
It is underneath the coppice and heath,
And the thin anemones.
Only the keeper sees
That, where the ring-dove broods,
And the badgers roll at ease,
There was once a road through the woods.
Yet, if you enter the woods
Of a summer evening late,
When the night-air cools on the trout-ringed pools
Where the otter whistles his mate,
(They fear not men in the woods,
Because they see so few.)
You will hear the beat of a horse's feet,
And the swish of a skirt in the dew,
Steadily cantering through
The misty solitudes,
As though they perfectly knew
The old lost road through the woods.
But there is no road through the woods ...

William Collins (1721–1759)

Ode to Evening

If aught of oaten stop, or past'ral song,
May hope, chaste Eve, to soothe thy modest ear,
    Like thy own solemn springs,
    Thy springs and dying gales,
O nymph reserved, while now the bright-haired sun
Sits in yon western tent, whose cloudy skirts,
    With brede ethereal wove,
    O'erhang his wavy bed;
Now air is hushed, save where the weak-ey'd bat
With short shrill shriek flits by on leathern wing,
    Or where the beetle winds
    His small but sullen horn
As oft he rises 'midst the twilight path
Against the pilgrim, borne in heedless hum:
    Now teach me, maid composed,
    To breathe some softened strain,
Whose numbers stealing through thy dark'ning vale
May not unseemly with its stillness suit,
    As musing slow, I hail
    Thy genial loved return.
For when thy folding star arising shows
His paly circlet, at his warning lamp
    The fragrant Hours, and elves
    Who slept in flowers the day,
And many a nymph who wreathes her brows with sedge
And sheds the fresh'ning dew, and lovelier still,
    The pensive pleasures sweet
    Prepare thy shad'wy car.
Then lead, calm votress, where some sheety lake

Cheers the lone heath, or some time-hallowed pile
   Or upland fallows grey
   Reflect its last cool gleam.
But when chill blust'ring winds, or driving rain,
Forbid my willing feet, be mine the hut
   That from the mountain's side
   Views wilds, and swelling floods,
And hamlets brown, and dim-discovered spires,
And hears their simple bell, and marks o'er all
   Thy dewy fingers draw
   The gradual dusky veil.
While Spring shall pour his showers, as oft he wont,
And bathe thy breathing tresses, meekest Eve;
   While Summer loves to sport
   Beneath thy ling'ring light;
While sallow Autumn fills thy lap with leaves;
Or Winter, yelling through the troublous air,
   Affrights thy shrinking train
   And rudely rends thy robes;
So long, sure-found beneath the sylvan shed,
Shall Fancy, Friendship, Science, rose-lipp'd Health,
   Thy gentlest influence own,
   And hymn thy fav'rite name!

Samuel Taylor Coleridge (1772–1834)

This Lime-Tree Bower My Prison

[Addressed to Charles Lamb, of the India House, London]

Well, they are gone, and here must I remain,
This lime-tree bower my prison! I have lost
Beauties and feelings, such as would have been
Most sweet to my remembrance even when age
Had dimmed mine eyes to blindness! They, meanwhile,
Friends, whom I never more may meet again,
On springy heath, along the hill-top edge,
Wander in gladness, and wind down, perchance,
To that still roaring dell, of which I told;
The roaring dell, o'er wooded, narrow deep,
And only speckled by the mid-day sun;
Where its slim trunk the ash from rock to rock
Flings arching like a bridge;—that branchless ash,
Unsunned and damp, whose few poor yellow leaves
Ne'er tremble in the gale, yet tremble still,
Fanned by the water-fall! and there my friends
Behold the dark green file of long lank weeds,
That all at once (a most fantastic sight!)
Still nod and drip beneath the dripping edge
Of the blue clay-stone.

                    Now, my friends emerge
Beneath the wide wide Heaven—and view again
The many-steepled tract magnificent
Of hilly fields and meadows, and the sea,
With some fair bark, perhaps, whose sails light up
The slip of smooth clear blue betwixt two Isles

Of purple shadow! Yes! they wander on
In gladness all; but thou, methinks, most glad,
My gentle-hearted Charles! for thou hast pined
And hungered after Nature, many a year,
In the great City pent, winning thy way
With sad yet patient soul, through evil and pain
And strange calamity! Ah! slowly sink
Behind the western ridge, thou glorious sun!
Shine in the slant beams of the sinking orb,
Ye purple heath-flowers! richlier burn, ye clouds!
Live in the yellow light, ye distant groves!
And kindle, thou blue ocean! So my Friend
Struck with deep joy may stand, as I have stood,
Silent with swimming sense; yea, gazing round
On the wide landscape, gaze till all doth seem
Less gross than bodily; and of such hues
As veil the Almighty Spirit, when yet he makes
Spirits perceive his presence.

       A delight
Comes sudden on my heart, and I am glad
As I myself were there! Nor in this bower,
This little lime-tree bower, have I not marked
Much that has soothed me. Pale beneath the blaze
Hung the transparent foliage; and I watched
Some broad and sunny leaf, and loved to see
The shadow of the leaf and stem above
Dappling its sunshine! And that walnut-tree
Was richly tinged, and a deep radiance lay
Full on the ancient ivy, which usurps
Those fronting elms, and now, with blackest mass
Makes their dark branches gleam a lighter hue
Through the late twilight: and though now the bat

Wheels silent by, and not a swallow twitters,
Yet still the solitary humble bee
Sings in the bean-flower! Henceforth, I shall know
That Nature ne'er deserts the wise and pure;
No plot so narrow, be but Nature there,
No waste so vacant, but may well employ
Each faculty of sense, and keep the heart
Awake to Love and Beauty! and sometimes
'Tis well to be bereft of promised good,
That we may lift the soul, and contemplate
With lively joy the joys we cannot share.
My gentle-hearted Charles! when the last rook
Beat its straight path along the dusky air
Homewards, I blessed it! deeming its black wing
(Now a dim speck, now vanishing in light)
Had crossed the mighty orb's dilated glory,
While thou stood'st gazing; or when all was still,
Flew creeking o'er thy head, and had a charm
For thee, my gentle-hearted Charles, to whom
No sound is dissonant which tells of Life.

William Roscoe (1753–1831)

The Butterfly's Ball and the Grasshopper's Feast

Come take up your Hats, and away let us haste
To the Butterfly's Ball, and the Grasshopper's Feast.
The Trumpeter, Gad-fly, has summon'd the Crew,
And the Revels are now only waiting for you.

So said little Robert, and pacing along,
His merry Companions came forth in a Throng.
And on the smooth Grass, by the side of a Wood,
Beneath a broad Oak that for Ages had stood,

Saw the Children of Earth, and the Tenants of Air,
For an Evening's Amusement together repair.
And there came the Beetle, so blind and so black,
Who carried the Emmet, his Friend, on his Back.

And there was the Gnat and the Dragon-fly too,
With all their Relations, Green, Orange, and Blue.
And there came the Moth, with his Plumage of Down,
And the Hornet in Jacket of Yellow and Brown;

Who with him the Wasp, his Companion, did bring,
But they promis'd, that Evening, to lay by their Sting.
And the sly little Dormouse crept out of his Hole,
And brought to the Feast his blind Brother, the Mole.

And the Snail, with his Horns peeping out of his Shell,
Came from a great Distance, the Length of an Ell.
A Mushroom their Table, and on it was laid
A Water-dock Leaf, which a Table-cloth made.

The Viands were various, to each of their Taste,
And the Bee brought her Honey to crown the Repast.
Then close on his Haunches, so solemn and wise,
The Frog from a Corner, look'd up to the Skies.

And the Squirrel well pleas'd such Diversions to see,
Mounted high over Head, and look'd down from a Tree.

Then out came the Spider, with Finger so fine,
To shew his Dexterity on the tight Line.

From one Branch to another, his Cobwebs he slung,
Then quick as an Arrow he darted along,
But just in the Middle, – Oh! shocking to tell,
From his Rope, in an Instant, poor Harlequin fell.

Yet he touch'd not the Ground, but with Talons outspread,
Hung suspended in Air, at the End of a Thread,
Then the Grasshopper came with a Jerk and a Spring,
Very long was his Leg, though but short was his Wing;

He took but three Leaps, and was soon out of Sight,
Then chirp'd his own Praises the rest of the Night.
With Step so majestic the Snail did advance,
And promis'd the Gazers a Minuet to dance.

But they all laugh'd so loud that he pull'd in his Head,
And went in his own little Chamber to Bed.
Then, as Evening gave Way to the Shadows of Night,
Their Watchman, the Glow-worm, came out with a Light.

Then Home let us hasten, while yet we can see,
For no Watchman is waiting for you and for me.
So said little Robert, and pacing along,
His merry Companions returned in a Throng.

Charles Cotton (1630–1687)

Evening Quatrains

The Day's grown old, the fainting Sun
Has but a little way to run,
And yet his Steeds, with all his skill,
Scarce lug the Chariot down the Hill.

With Labour spent, and Thirst opprest,
Whilst they strain hard to gain the West,
From Fetlocks hot drops melted light,
Which turn to Meteors in the Night.

The Shadows now so long do grow,
That Brambles like tall Cedars show,
Mole-hills seem Mountains, and the Ant
Appears a monstrous Elephant.

A very little little Flock
Shades thrice the ground that it would stock;
Whilst the small Stripling following them,
Appears a mighty Polypheme.

These being brought into the Fold,
And by the thrifty Master told,
He thinks his Wages are well paid,
Since none are either lost, or stray'd.

Now lowing Herds are each-where heard,
Chains rattle in the Villeins Yard,
The Cart's on Tayl set down to rest,
Bearing on high the Cuckolds Crest.

The hedg is stript, the Clothes brought in,
Nought's left without should be within,
The Bees are hiv'd, and hum their Charm,
Whilst every House does seem a Swarm.

The Cock now to the Roost is prest:
For he must call up all the rest;
The Sow's fast pegg'd within the Sty,
To still her squeaking Progeny.

Each one has had his Supping Mess,
The Cheese is put into the Press,
The Pans and Bowls clean scalded all,
Rear'd up against the Milk-house Wall.

And now on Benches all are sat
In the cool Air to sit and chat,
Till Phoebus, dipping in the West,
Shall lead the World the way to Rest.

George Meredith (1828–1909)

We saw the swallows gathering in the sky

Meredith posed as the tragic young poet for Henry's Wallis's famous painting The Death of Chatterton, *though he must have regretted doing so because his wife eloped with Wallis shortly afterwards. He remarried and settled in Surrey, where the countryside inspired much of his subsequent writing.*

We saw the swallows gathering in the sky,
And in the osier-isle we heard them noise.
We had not to look back on summer joys,
Or forward to a summer of bright dye:
But in the largeness of the evening earth
Our spirits grew as we went side by side.
The hour became her husband and my bride.
Love that had robbed us so, thus blessed our dearth!
The pilgrims of the year waxed very loud
In multitudinous chatterings, as the flood
Full brown came from the West, and like pale blood
Expanded to the upper crimson cloud.
Love that had robbed us of immortal things,
This little moment mercifully gave,
Where I have seen across the twilight wave
The swan sail with her young beneath her wings.

John Betjeman (1906–1984)

Lake District

I pass the cruet and I see the lake
   Running with light, beyond the garden pine,
    That lake whose waters make me dream her mine.
Up to the top board mounting for my sake,
For me she breathes, for me each soft intake,
   For me the plunge, the lake and limbs combine.
   I pledge her in non-alcoholic wine
And give the H.P. Sauce another shake.

Spirit of Grasmere, bells of Ambleside,
   Sing you and ring you, water bells, for me;
    You water-colour waterfalls may froth.
Long hiking holidays will yet provide
   Long stony lanes and back at six to tea
    And Heinz's ketchup on the tablecloth.

John Milton (1608–1674)

Lycidas [extract]

Now, Lycidas, the shepherds weep no more;
Henceforth thou art the Genius of the shore,
In thy large recompense, and shalt be good
To all that wander in that perilous flood.
    Thus sang the uncouth swain to the oaks and rills,
While the still morn went out with sandals grey;
He touched the tender stops of various quills,
With eager thought warbling his Doric lay.
And now the sun had stretched out all the hills,
And now was dropped into the western bay;
At last he rose, and twitched his mantle blue:
Tomorrow to fresh woods, and pastures new.

WINTER

The hushed beauty of the British countryside beneath a fresh snowfall can ignite a childlike excitement in even the most mature observer. The poets gathered here have both celebrated the exhilaration of bitterly cold days and lamented the bleakness of the land during a harsh winter. Short days and long freezing nights have evidently provided much time for contemplation and composition through the centuries.

Thomas Hood (1799–1845)

No!

No sun – no moon!
No morn – no noon!
No dawn – no dusk – no proper time of day –
No sky – no earthly view –
No distance looking blue –
No road – no street – no 't'other side this way' –
No end to any Row –
No indications where the Crescents go –
No top to any steeple –
No recognitions of familiar people –
No courtesies for showing 'em –
No knowing 'em!
No travelling at all – no locomotion –
No inkling of the way – no notion –
'No go' by land or ocean –
No mail – no post –
No news from any foreign coast –
No Park, no Ring, no afternoon gentility –
No company – no nobility –
No warmth, no cheerfulness, no healthful ease,
No comfortable feel in any member –
No shade, no shine, no butterflies, no bees,
No fruits, no flowers, no leaves, no birds –
November!

William Wordsworth (1770–1850)

The Prelude [extract]

And in the frosty season, when the sun
Was set, and visible for many a mile
The cottage windows blazed through twilight gloom,
I heeded not their summons: happy time
It was indeed for all of us – for me
It was a time of rapture! Clear and loud
The village clock tolled six; I wheeled about,
Proud and exulting like an untired horse
That cares not for his home. All shod with steel,
We hissed along the polished ice in games
Confederate, imitative of the chase
And woodland pleasures – the resounding horn,
The pack loud chiming, and the hunted hare.
So through the darkness and the cold we flew,
And not a voice was idle; with the din
Smitten, the precipices rang aloud;
The leafless trees and every icy crag
Tinkled like iron; while far distant hills
Into the tumult sent an alien sound
Of melancholy not unnoticed, while the stars,
Eastward, were sparkling clear, and in the west
The orange sky of evening died away.
Not seldom from the uproar I retired
Into a silent bay, or sportively
Glanced sideway, leaving the tumultuous throng,
To cut across the reflex of a star
That fled, and, flying still before me, gleamed
Upon the glassy plain; and oftentimes,
When we had given our bodies to the wind,

And all the shadowy banks on either side
Came sweeping through the darkness, spinning still
The rapid line of motion, then at once
Have I, reclining back upon my heels,
Stopped short; yet still the solitary cliffs
Wheeled by me – even as if the earth had rolled
With visible motion her diurnal round!
Behind me did they stretch in solemn train,
Feebler and feebler, and I stood and watched
Till all was tranquil as a dreamless sleep.

Thomas Hardy (1840–1928)

The Darkling Thrush

I leant upon a coppice gate
    When Frost was spectre-grey,
And Winter's dregs made desolate
    The weakening eye of day.
The tangled bine-stems scored the sky
    Like strings of broken lyres,
And all mankind that haunted nigh
    Had sought their household fires.

The land's sharp features seemed to be
    The Century's corpse outleant,
His crypt the cloudy canopy,
    The wind his death-lament.
The ancient pulse of germ and birth
    Was shrunken hard and dry,
And every spirit upon earth
    Seemed fervourless as I.

At once a voice arose among
    The bleak twigs overhead
In a full-hearted evensong
    Of joy illimited;
An aged thrush, frail, gaunt, and small,
    In blast-beruffled plume,
Had chosen thus to fling his soul
    Upon the growing gloom.

So little cause for carolings
    Of such ecstatic sound
Was written on terrestrial things
    Afar or nigh around,
That I could think there trembled through
    His happy good-night air
Some blessed Hope, whereof he knew
    And I was unaware.

Samuel Taylor Coleridge (1772–1834)

Frost at Midnight

Coleridge promises his son a country upbringing of the kind he lacked and longed for, having spent his own childhood in the city. Much of the imagery evokes the Lake District, the part of Britain that most inspired and delighted Coleridge, Wordsworth and their contemporaries.

    The Frost performs its secret ministry,
Unhelped by any wind. The owlet's cry
Came loud—and hark, again! loud as before.
The inmates of my cottage, all at rest,

Have left me to that solitude, which suits
Abstruser musings: save that at my side
My cradled infant slumbers peacefully.
'Tis calm indeed! so calm, that it disturbs
And vexes meditation with its strange
And extreme silentness. Sea, hill, and wood,
This populous village! Sea, and hill, and wood,
With all the numberless goings-on of life,
Inaudible as dreams! the thin blue flame
Lies on my low-burnt fire, and quivers not;
Only that film, which fluttered on the grate,
Still flutters there, the sole unquiet thing.
Methinks, its motion in this hush of nature
Gives it dim sympathies with me who live,
Making it a companionable form,
Whose puny flaps and freaks the idling Spirit
By its own moods interprets, every where
Echo or mirror seeking of itself,
And makes a toy of Thought.

                             But O! how oft,
How oft, at school, with most believing mind,
Presageful, have I gazed upon the bars,
To watch that fluttering stranger! and as oft
With unclosed lids, already had I dreamt
Of my sweet birthplace, and the old church tower,
Whose bells, the poor man's only music, rang
From morn to evening, all the hot Fair-day,
So sweetly, that they stirred and haunted me
With a wild pleasure, falling on mine ear
Most like articulate sounds of things to come!
So gazed I, till the soothing things, I dreamt,
Lulled me to sleep, and sleep prolonged my dreams!

And so I brooded all the following morn,
Awed by the stern preceptor's face, mine eye
Fixed with mock study on my swimming book:
Save if the door half opened, and I snatched
A hasty glance, and still my heart leaped up,
For still I hoped to see the stranger's face,
Townsman, or aunt, or sister more beloved,
My playmate when we both were clothed alike!

Dear Babe, that sleepest cradled by my side,
Whose gentle breathings, heard in this deep calm,
Fill up the interspersèd vacancies
And momentary pauses of the thought!
My babe so beautiful! it thrills my heart
With tender gladness, thus to look at thee,
And think that thou shalt learn far other lore,
And in far other scenes! For I was reared
In the great city, pent 'mid cloisters dim,
And saw nought lovely but the sky and stars.
But thou, my babe! shalt wander like a breeze
By lakes and sandy shores, beneath the crags
Of ancient mountain, and beneath the clouds,
Which image in their bulk both lakes and shores
And mountain crags: so shalt thou see and hear
The lovely shapes and sounds intelligible
Of that eternal language, which thy God
Utters, who from eternity doth teach
Himself in all, and all things in himself.
Great universal Teacher! he shall mould
Thy spirit, and by giving make it ask.

Therefore all seasons shall be sweet to thee,
Whether the summer clothe the general earth
With greenness, or the redbreast sit and sing
Betwixt the tufts of snow on the bare branch
Of mossy apple tree, while the nigh thatch
Smokes in the sun-thaw; whether the eave-drops fall
Heard only in the trances of the blast,
Or if the secret ministry of frost
Shall hang them up in silent icicles,
Quietly shining to the quiet Moon.

Gerard Manley Hopkins (1844–1889)

Winter

The times are nightfall, look, their light grows less;
The times are winter, watch, a world undone:
They waste, they wither worse; they as they run
Or bring more or more blazon man's distress.
And I not help. Nor word now of success:
All is from wreck, here, there, to rescue one—
Work which to see scarce so much as begun
Makes welcome death, does dear forgetfulness.

Or what is else? There is your world within.
There rid the dragons, root out there the sin.
Your will is law in that small commonweal …

Christopher Smart (1722–1770)

A Song to David [extract]

An almost certainly apocryphal tale has Smart scratching A Song to
David *with a key into the wall of the mental asylum where he was being
confined. Though this is unlikely, the poem was probably written during
his internment.*

The cheerful holly, pensive yew,
And holy thorn, their trim renew;
  The squirrel hoards his nuts;
All creatures batten o'er their stores,
And careful nature all her doors
  For adoration shuts.

****

The laurels with the winter strive;
The crocus burnishes alive
  Upon the snow-clad earth;
For adoration myrtles stay
To keep the garden from dismay,
  And bless the sight from dearth.

Charles Tomlinson (1927–)

Saving the Appearances

The horse is white. Or it
appears to be under this
November light that could
well be October. It goes
as nimbly as a spider does
but it is gainly: the great
field makes it small
so that it seems
to crawl out of the distance
and to grow not larger
but less slow. Stains
on its sides show where
the mud is and the power
now overmasters the fragility
of its earlier bearing. Tall
it shudders over one and bends
a full neck, cropping
the foreground, blotting
the whole space back
behind those pounding feet.
Mounted, one feels the sky
as much the measure of the event
as the field had been, and all
the divisions of the indivisible
unite again, or seem
to do as when the approaching
horse was white, on this
November unsombre day
where what appears, is.

William Blake (1757–1827)

To Winter

O Winter! bar thine adamantine doors:
The north is thine; there hast thou built thy dark
Deep-founded habitation. Shake not thy roofs,
Nor bend thy pillars with thine iron car.

He hears me not, but o'er the yawning deep
Rides heavy; his storms are unchain'd; sheathed
In ribbed steel, I dare not lift mine eyes;
For he hath rear'd his sceptre o'er the world.

Lo! now the direful monster, whose skin clings
To his strong bones, strides o'er the groaning rocks:
He withers all in silence, and his hand
Unclothes the earth, and freezes up frail life.

He takes his seat upon the cliffs, the mariner
Cries in vain. Poor little wretch! that deal'st
With storms; till heaven smiles, and the monster
Is driven yelling to his caves beneath Mount Hecla.

Alfred, Lord Tennyson (1809–1892)

In Memoriam A.H.H. [extract]

Dip down upon the northern shore,
  O sweet new-year delaying long;
  Thou dost expectant nature wrong;
Delaying long, delay no more.

What stays thee from the clouded noons,
  Thy sweetness from its proper place?
  Can trouble live with April days,
Or sadness in the summer moons?

Bring orchis, bring the foxglove spire,
  The little speedwell's darling blue,
  Deep tulips dashed with fiery dew,
Laburnums, dropping-wells of fire.

O thou, new-year, delaying long,
  Delayest the sorrow in my blood,
  That longs to burst a frozen bud
And flood a fresher throat with song.

T.S. Eliot (1888–1965)

Little Gidding [extract]

Midwinter spring is its own season
Sempiternal though sodden towards sundown,
Suspended in time, between pole and tropic.
When the short day is brightest, with frost and fire,
The brief sun flames the ice, on pond and ditches,
In windless cold that is the heart's heat,
Reflecting in a watery mirror
A glare that is blindness in the early afternoon.
And glow more intense than blaze of branch, or brazier,
Stirs the dumb spirit: no wind, but pentecostal fire
In the dark time of the year. Between melting and freezing
The soul's sap quivers. There is no earth smell
Or smell of living thing. This is the spring time
But not in time's covenant. Now the hedgerow
Is blanched for an hour with transitory blossom
Of snow, a bloom more sudden
Than that of summer, neither budding nor fading,
Not in the scheme of generation.
Where is the summer, the unimaginable
Zero summer?

James Thomson (1700–1748)

The Seasons [extract]

The lyrics to 'Rule Britannia' are the Scottish Thomson's best-known work.

Through the hushed air the whitening shower descends,
At first thin-wavering; till at last the flakes
Fall broad and wide and fast, dimming the day,
With a continual flow. The cherished fields
Put on their winter robe of purest white.
'Tis brightness all; save where the new snow melts
Along the mazy current. Low the woods
Bow their hoar heads; and, ere the languid sun
Faint from the west emits his evening ray,
Earth's universal face, deep-hid and chill,
Is one wild, dazzling waste.

Edward Thomas (1878–1917)

The Manor Farm

Thomas was always entranced by the countryside and spent much of his city childhood walking on the commons of South London. Later, he lived in rural Kent and Hampshire and nature became a key theme in his prose essays as well as poetry.

The rock-like mud unfroze a little and rills
Ran and sparkled down each side of the road
Under the catkins wagging in the hedge.

But earth would have her sleep out, spite of the sun;
Nor did I value that thin glilding beam
More than a pretty February thing
Till I came down to the old Manor Farm,
And church and yew-tree opposite, in age
Its equals and in size. The church and yew
And farmhouse slept in a Sunday silentness.
The air raised not a straw. The steep farm roof,
With tiles duskily glowing, entertained
The mid-day sun; and up and down the roof
White pigeons nestled. There was no sound but one.
Three cart-horses were looking over a gate
Drowsily through their forelocks, swishing their tails
Against a fly, a solitary fly.

The Winter's cheek flushed as if he had drained
Spring, Summer, and Autumn at a draught
And smiled quietly. But 'twas not Winter –
Rather a season of bliss unchangeable
Awakened from farm and church where it had lain
Safe under tile and thatch for ages since
This England, Old already, was called Merry.

Night

Today, it is only in the countryside that true night – the land lit by the moon and stars instead of by streetlights – can be witnessed. In the deep darkness, senses are sharpened: sounds are amplified and shadows shape-shift. Even the most familiar landscape can take on an eerie strangeness when seen bathed in moonlight. It seems appropriate to close this collection with works inspired by rambles in the rural darkness.

Vita Sackville-West (1892–1962)

The Land [extract]

Now in the radiant night no men are stirring:
The little houses sleep with shuttered panes;
Only the hares are wakeful, loosely loping
Along the hedges with their easy gait,
And big loose ears, and pad-prints crossing snow;
The ricks and trees stand silent in the moon,
Loaded with snow, and tiny drifts from branches
Slip to the ground in woods with sliding sigh.
Private the woods, enjoying a secret beauty.

William Blake (1757–1827)

To the Evening Star

Thou fair-haired angel of the evening,
Now, while the sun rests on the mountains, light
Thy bright torch of love; thy radiant crown
Put on, and smile upon our evening bed!
Smile on our loves, and while thou drawest the
Blue curtains of the sky, scatter thy silver dew
On every flower that shuts its sweet eyes
In timely sleep. Let thy west wind sleep on
The lake; speak silence with thy glimmering eyes,
And wash the dusk with silver. Soon, full soon,
Dost thou withdraw; then the wolf rages wide,
And the lion glares through the dun forest.
The fleeces of our flocks are covered with
Thy sacred dew; protect with them with thine influence.

Matthew Arnold (1822–1888)

Dover Beach

Arnold's work as a schools' inspector saw him crisscross the countryside
on the new Victorian railway network, and gave him a familiarity with
the British outdoors many of his metropolitan literary peers lacked.

The sea is calm tonight.
The tide is full, the moon lies fair
Upon the straits; on the French coast the light
Gleams and is gone; the cliffs of England stand,
Glimmering and vast, out in the tranquil bay.
Come to the window, sweet is the night-air!

Only, from the long line of spray
Where the sea meets the moon-blanched land,
Listen! you hear the grating roar
Of pebbles which the waves draw back, and fling,
At their return, up the high strand,
Begin, and cease, and then again begin,
With tremulous cadence slow, and bring
The eternal note of sadness in.

Sophocles long ago
Heard it on the Aegean, and it brought
Into his mind the turbid ebb and flow
Of human misery; we
Find also in the sound a thought,
Hearing it by this distant northern sea.

The Sea of Faith
Was once, too, at the full, and round earth's shore

Lay like the folds of a bright girdle furled.
But now I only hear
Its melancholy, long, withdrawing roar,
Retreating, to the breath
Of the night-wind, down the vast edges drear
And naked shingles of the world.

Ah, love, let us be true
To one another! for the world, which seems
To lie before us like a land of dreams,
So various, so beautiful, so new,
Hath really neither joy, nor love, nor light,
Nor certitude, nor peace, nor help for pain;
And we are here as on a darkling plain
Swept with confused alarms of struggle and flight,
Where ignorant armies clash by night.

Jean Ingelow (1820–1897)

The Long White Seam

As I came round the harbour buoy,
     The lights began to gleam,
No wave the land-locked water stirred,
     The crags were white as cream;
And I marked my love by candle-light
     Sewing her long white seam.
          It's aye sewing ashore, my dear,
               Watch and steer at sea,
          It's reef and furl, and haul the line,
               Set sail and think of thee.

I climbed to reach her cottage door;
 O sweetly my love sings!
Like a shaft of light her voice breaks forth,
 My soul to meet it springs
As the shining water leaped of old,
 When stirred by angel wings.
  Aye longing to list anew,
   Awake and in my dream,
But never a song she sang like this,
Sewing her long white seam.

Fair fall the lights, the harbour lights,
 That brought me in to thee,
And peace drop down on that low roof
 For the sight that I did see,
And the voice, my dear, that rang so clear
 All for the love of me.
  For O, for O, with brows bent low
   By the candle's flickering gleam,
   Her wedding gown it was she wrought,
    Sewing the long white seam.

Edward Thomas (1878–1917)

Out in the Dark

Out in the dark over the snow
The fallow fawns invisible go
With the fallow doe;
And the winds blow
Fast as the stars are slow.

Stealthily the dark haunts round
And, when the lamp goes, without sound
At a swifter bound
Than the swiftest hound,
Arrives, and all else is drowned;

And star and I and wind and deer,
Are in the dark together, – near,
Yet far, – and fear
Drums on my ear
In the sage company drear.

How weak and little is the light,
All the universe of sight,
Love and delight,
Before the might,
If you love it not, of night.

Alfred, Lord Tennyson (1809–1892)

The Owl

Of all the night's creatures, the owl has perhaps the most evocative cry.

When cats run home and light is come,
   And dew is cold upon the ground,
And the far-off stream is dumb,
   And the whirring sail goes round,
   And the whirring sail goes round;
     Alone and warming his five wits,
     The white owl in the belfry sits.

When merry milkmaids click the latch,
   And rarely smells the new-mown hay,
And the cock hath sung beneath the thatch
   Twice or thrice his roundelay,
   Twice or thrice his roundelay;
     Alone and warming his five wits,
     The white owl in the belfry sits.

Walter de la Mare (1873–1956)

Silver

De la Mare was evidently inspired by the night. As well as this much-loved poem, he produced a number of ghost stories.

Slowly, silently, now the moon
Walks the night in her silver shoon;
This way, and that, she peers, and sees
Silver fruit upon silver trees;
One by one the casements catch
Her beams beneath the silvery thatch;
Couched in his kennel, like a log,
With paws of silver sleeps the dog;
From their shadowy cote the white breasts peep
Of doves in a silver-feathered sleep;
A harvest mouse goes scampering by,
With silver claws, and silver eye;
And moveless fish in the water gleam,
By silver reeds in a silver stream.

Select Bibliography

Barber, Laura *Penguin's Poems for Life* (Penguin Classics, 2008)

Betjeman, John *Collected Poems* (John Murray, 2006)

Blake, William *Selected Poems* (Penguin Classics, 2005)

Bradley, Margaret (Ed.) *More Poetry Please! 100 Popular Poems from the BBC Radio 4 Programme* (J. M. Dent, 1988)

Carr, Samuel *Ode to the Countryside* (National Trust, 2010)

Creighton, T.R.N. (Ed.) *Poems of Thomas Hardy, A New Selection* (Macmillan, 1974)

Ferguson, Margaret; Salter, Mary Jo; Stallworthy, Jon (Eds) *The Norton Anthology of Poetry* (Fifth Edition) (Norton, 2005)

Housman, A. E. *The Collected Poems of A. E. Housman* (Wordsworth Editions, 1994)

Hydes, Jack (Ed.) *Touched with Fire: An Anthology of Poems* (Cambridge University Press, 1985)

Ricks, Christopher (Ed.) *The Oxford Book of English Verse* (Oxford University Press, 1999)

Roe, Dinah (Ed.) *The Pre-Raphaelites: From Rossetti to Ruskin* (Penguin Classics, 2010)

Sampson, Ana (Ed.) *I Wandered Lonely as a Cloud ...: and other poems you half-remember from school* (Michael O'Mara, 2009)

Sampson, Ana (Ed.) *Tyger Tyger Burning Bright: Much-Loved Poems You Half-Remember* (Michael O'Mara, 2011)

Sheers, Owen *A Poet's Guide to Britain* (Penguin Classics, 2009)

Tennyson, Alfred, Lord *Selected Poetry* (Penguin, 1941)

Thomas, Dylan *Collected Poems 1934–1952* (Phoenix, 2000)

Thomas, Edward *Collected Poems* (Faber & Faber, 2004)

Acknowledgements

The author and publishers are grateful to the following for permission to use material that is in copyright:

Matthew Arnold: 'Dover Beach' and an extract from 'The Scholar Gypsy' reproduced by kind permission of Frederick Whitridge.

W. H. Auden: 'On This Island' copyright © 1936, 1938, 1940 renewed. Reprinted by permission of Curtis Brown, Ltd.

John Betjeman: 'A Bay in Anglesey', 'Autumn 1964' and 'Lake District' from *Collected Poems* by John Betjeman © The Estate of John Betjeman 1955, 1958, 1962, 1964, 1968, 1970, 1979, 1981, 1982, 2001. Reproduced by permission of John Murray (Publishers) Limited.

Frances Cornford: 'The Coast: Norfolk' reproduced with the permission of the trustees of the Frances Crofts Cornford Will Trust.

Donald Davie: 'The Mushroom Gatherers' and 'Tunstall Forest' from *Collected Poems* (Carcanet, 1990) reprinted by permission of Carcanet Press Limited.

Walter de la Mare: 'Silver' reprinted by permission of the Literary Trustees of Walter de la Mare and The Society of Authors as their representative.

T.S. Eliot: 'Little Gidding' extract taken from *The Complete Poems and Plays* (Faber and Faber) and reprinted by permission of Faber and Faber Limited.

Edwin Muir: 'Childhood' from *Collected Poems* (Faber and Faber) reprinted by permission of Faber and Faber Limited.

Vita Sackville-West: Extracts from *The Land* (Heinemann, 1939) reprinted by permission of Curtis Brown, Ltd.

Samuel Taylor Coleridge: 'Frost at Midnight' and 'This Lime-Tree Bower My Prison' reproduced by kind permission of Mrs Priscilla Coleridge Cassam.

Dylan Thomas: 'Fern Hill', 'Poem in October' and 'We Lying by Seasand' from *Collected Poems: Dylan Thomas* (Phoenix) reprinted by permission of David Higham Associates Limited.

Edward Thomas: 'Adelstrop', 'July', 'October', 'Out in the Dark', 'The Glory', 'The Lane' and 'The Manor Farm' by Edward Thomas reproduced by kind permission of Rosemary Vellender.

Charles Tomlinson: 'Saving the Appearances' from *Selected Poems* (OUP, 1997) reprinted by permission of Carcanet Press Limited.

Siegfried Sassoon: 'Wind in the Beechwood' by Siegfried Sassoon. Copyright Siegfried Sassoon by kind permission of the Estate of George Sassoon.

Index of Poets

Index of Titles, First Lines and Well-Known Lines

Titles of poems are in **bold** type, first lines are in roman type, and familiar or well-known lines are in *italic* type following a headword in ***bold italics***.